T0380316

COME EARLY, STAY LATE

LIFE IN THE TRENCHES OF SMALL GROUP MINISTRY

DR. JAY SLIFE

WESTBOW
PRESS®
A DIVISION OF THOMAS NELSON
& ZONDERVAN

Copyright © 2024 Dr. Jay Slife.

All rights reserved. No part of this book may be used or reproduced by any means, graphic, electronic, or mechanical, including photocopying, recording, taping or by any information storage retrieval system without the written permission of the author except in the case of brief quotations embodied in critical articles and reviews.

This book is a work of non-fiction. Unless otherwise noted, the author and the publisher make no explicit guarantees as to the accuracy of the information contained in this book and in some cases, names of people and places have been altered to protect their privacy.

WestBow Press books may be ordered through booksellers or by contacting:

WestBow Press
A Division of Thomas Nelson & Zondervan
1663 Liberty Drive
Bloomington, IN 47403
www.westbowpress.com
844-714-3454

Because of the dynamic nature of the Internet, any web addresses or links contained in this book may have changed since publication and may no longer be valid. The views expressed in this work are solely those of the author and do not necessarily reflect the views of the publisher, and the publisher hereby disclaims any responsibility for them.

Any people depicted in stock imagery provided by Getty Images are models, and such images are being used for illustrative purposes only. Certain stock imagery © Getty Images.

Scripture taken from the Holy Bible, NEW INTERNATIONAL VERSION®. Copyright © 1973, 1978, 1984, 2011 by Biblica, Inc. All rights reserved worldwide. Used by permission. NEW INTERNATIONAL VERSION® and NIV® are registered trademarks of Biblica, Inc. Use of either trademark for the offering of goods or services requires the prior written consent of Biblica US, Inc.

Scripture quotations taken from the New American Standard Bible®, Copyright © 1960, 1962, 1963, 1968, 1971, 1972, 1973, 1975, 1977, 1995 by The Lockman Foundation. Used by permission. (www.Lockman.org)

Scripture taken from the King James Version of the Bible.

Scripture taken from the Amplified Bible, copyright © 1954, 1958, 1962, 1964, 1965, 1987 by The Lockman Foundation. Used by permission.

Scripture taken from the New King James Version. Copyright © 1979, 1980, 1982 by Thomas Nelson, Inc. Used by permission. All rights reserved.

ISBN: 979-8-3850-2421-6 (sc)
ISBN: 979-8-3850-2422-3 (hc)
ISBN: 979-8-3850-2423-0 (e)

Library of Congress Control Number: 2024908094

Print information available on the last page.

WestBow Press rev. date: 6/3/2024

DEDICATION

This book is dedicated to Jesus, my Lord and King. Yes, this is my story. But this is actually more his story than mine. He is the one who has walked with and directed me through all of life. He is the one who invited me to be his friend -- but then had teach me how! He is the one who has been so overwhelmingly patient, kind, and faithful. Thank you, Father, for all that you do and are. May this book bring glory to you, and gain to all those who engage you in its reading.

ACKNOWLEDGMENT

I cannot claim full credit for the writing of this book. It would not have come together at all without the many hours of investment into me and it made by my daughter, Kristi. We do enjoy the art of banter once in a while. In that context, I have said that she is second only to Webster in her command of the English language and its grammar, a statement much truer than not! And she has said that she is the Captain of the Grammar Police! And has "arrested" me more times than I can count!

You are an amazing person, Kristi Lynn. I am very blessed to have you as my daughter. And also very blessed by your willing heart to help me as you have. Thank you, from my heart to yours.

CONTENTS

Introduction..xi

**PART ONE: AN EXPOSITION ON THE CURRENT STATE
OF AFFAIRS WITHIN THE CHURCH AT LARGE**

Chapter 1   Sally and Annie 1
Chapter 2   Anticipate the Lord's Moving.................................9
Chapter 3   Solution One: Submit to the Lordship of Jesus....... 17
Chapter 4   Solution Two: Align with his Word.......................28
Chapter 5   Solution Three: Identifying That Which
             Stands in the Way.......................................36
Chapter 6   Solution Four: Understanding Your Purpose..........44

**PART TWO: THE NEW TESTAMENT MODEL: THE
ARGUMENT FOR HOUSE CHURCHES**

Chapter 7   The Assumption of the Kingdom of God 53
Chapter 8   The Argument for House Churches.......................66
Chapter 9   What is a Home Gathering?................................. 76
Chapter 10   Sunago: The Heart of it All 91

PART THREE: THE PRACTICS: THIS IS WHERE WE LIVE!

Chapter 11   Cultivating an Arena of Trust 101
Chapter 12   The Four Elements 106
Chapter 13   The How-To of Interactive Teaching.................... 112
Chapter 14   The What's and Why's of Spiritual Gifts 117
Chapter 15   The Essence of Leading a Home Gathering 127

Chapter 16 On Vocational Leadership 140
Chapter 17 To Those Starting Again or Being Shifted by
            God 144
Chapter 18 Essential Principles.. 151
Chapter 19 Thoughts and Insights from the Trenches........... 176

End Notes... 185

INTRODUCTION

There is something within me - and I think within the hearts of many others - the likes of which I have yet to fully define or even understand. It's a gnawing, a knowing, and a sensing. It's heavy at times. It's confusing at times. It's mostly unfulfilled. It's a burden, a directive given by God, although that does not describe it adequately. It's a calling to a ministry that is full of wonder and grace, power and delight, mercy and truth. It's based on the richness of past experiences and the promises of future glory. It has strength and depth, character and integrity, opulence and magnificence. It's the Lord's, and however one might describe it, it is a journey that is about to come forth in this time in history. In my life and yours.

I was six months old in the Lord when the leader of the small group we were attending asked me to take over the teaching and leadership of the group. He was not leaving. He saw something in me that I had not yet recognized: the spiritual gifts of leadership, teaching, and preaching. He was simply healthy enough to not have to lead. That was now well over 40 years ago. I have been building, leading, multiplying, and investing into small groups of one variety or another ever since. **This book is that story.**

A few years later, having been directed to a different church, my wife, Julia, and I were invited to take on the leadership of a mostly defunct singles group. We knew what seemed like absolutely nothing about developing small group ministry at that time, and neither did anyone else around us. It was quite an adventure! One of the initial questions we asked each other was, "Why would a few single folks want a married couple with children as leaders?" We quickly learned the answer to that question.

We led that group for several years and enjoyed some very delightful relationships with the people that came and went. The learning curve was steep in the early days. Holy Spirit proved himself faithful, even (perhaps especially) in the midst of my many shortcomings, as week after week he taught me much about the many dynamics of leading a small group. Often, he would download a teaching or a directive word totally different than the one I had prepared. From this I learned to listen. I learned to follow his lead.

That season, although we did not know it then, was prophetic in a number of ways. We have spent much of our time in ministry, from then until now, wrapped around and connected to some dimension of small groups. This book is the story of the many things the Lord has taught us through those groups. It brings me to tears to think about where we are today. Tears of joy, tears of amazement and wonder over the goodness and patience and faithfulness of our Lord and King.

At the same time that we entered into the singles group, I was in Bible college full-time, working as a service manager in an independent auto repair business full-time, and trying to figure out how to be a husband and dad to my wife and children full-time. Oh, and Julia was pregnant with number three! I was also blessed with the opportunity to preach every other Sunday morning at the assisted living home down the street from the church and every third Sunday evening at church. To say we were busy was quite an understatement!

My gift mix and my personality lend themselves to being very prophetic. In those days I saw things as very black or white with very little grace or mercy mixed in! My calling is to teach, preach, and prophesy – and I took full advantage of all of the above to duly thrash the masses with where they were not living in their walk with God. Of course, the truths I was professing were aimed totally at them and most certainly not at me, since I had arrived at perfection and was above reproach. ;-)

On one particular evening, after I finished waxing eloquent on some subject I have long since forgotten, one of the elders of the church approached me. She and her husband were of very sweet spirit, having walked with Jesus in missionary work for most of their lives. They were spiritual parents for us in those days. She called me out and said something that was so amazingly profound it flew right past me. It took me years to fully capture it. She said, "Jay, you need to learn something. You need to understand that God is interested in three things. He is interested in relationship, he is interested in relationship, and he is interested in relationship." Throughout my journey I have come to understand that statement very well.

All of life, all of the things the Lord has done and is doing for us, is about relationship, and is found within relationship. He created us for relationship. We are here to worship him, an act and expression of relationship. He, his Son, and Holy Spirit are one. That is relationship. He intends that we become the bride of his Son, Jesus, the Christ. That is relationship. Jesus came for us, died for us, and sent his Holy Spirit for us. Again, all in the realm of relationship. The Pharisees asked Jesus what was the greatest commandment. His response? You guessed it: Relationship. "Love the Lord your God with all your heart and with all your soul and with all your mind and with all your strength." Then Jesus, as he often did, seized the moment to teach and went on: "And the second is like it: Love your neighbor as yourself." (Mark 12:30; Matthew 22:39) Relationship. There has been a plethora of opportunities and encounters with the Lord, for myself and others, along this walk with him. All with the intention of helping us grow and better understand the depth and breadth of this truth.

As we developed understanding and formulated strategies and structures for the implementation of all we were learning, I found myself making a particular statement in the midst of invitations. I started to say, **"Come early, stay late,"** as a way of expressing my heart for the rendezvous with others. I was saying, "The door is open." To my house, to the place of meeting, to my home, to my heart. I was asking for people to open up; to engage with me, and me them, and together with the Lord. Because that is why we were created. Thus, the title of this book.

When we came to the place of fluidity in relationships, in small groups or big, in church or in the general stream of life, our hearts opened. We caught it! We understood why Jesus called the love for God and those all around us the greatest commandment. It is where he is found. It is where he dwells, where he thrives. His heart aches for time with you, with your family and friends. He longs for relationship with you. (Isaiah 30:18) Where two or more are gathered, he is there to be found. (Matthew 18:20) That is because he loves relationship and looks and longs for opportunities for just that!

It is my hope and prayer that you too will capture and be captured by the sweet beauty of relationship discovered in the midst of this journey we call life. I have found my Lord to be ever gentle, ever kind, never wavering in his love. I have found him trusting me way beyond where it was safe to do so, because he loves me and has great confidence in me. I have found his love to be beyond measure, his patience never-ending, his grace and mercy totally overwhelming. He never stops giving and loving. I have said to my Julia many times, "My love for you is way beyond expression – but I will spend the rest of my life trying!" (She likes that!) And so it is with my Lord; his love is way beyond my ability to capture, to embrace, to receive, to emulate – but I will spend the rest of my days trying. Trying to imprison it and be imprisoned by it, to understand it, and simply to receive and walk in it. And he spends his days pouring out that love on me.

The folks in that single's group took us on for one reason. They were not able to clearly define it early on, but it was evident. They were looking for an adventure, a journey we could all walk together. They were crying out for relationship. With Jesus. With us. With each other and those all around. We all want and need strong, healthy, Christ-centered, interactive, inter-dependent relationships. It is not good for man to be alone; nor woman, nor child. (Genesis 2:18) We have been created with the relationship bug in our inner being.

I am writing this book for two reasons. One has to do with the burden that has been placed upon me to disciple those who know Jesus and help them give what they have away to others - so that they too may get the message, the truth of Jesus, and live it out. In this comes the stark reality of relationships in all their fullness, vertical and horizontal.

The other reason has all to do with helping leaders, at any level, those already in the mix and those just called, to make the shift, the transition, to the _biblical pattern of ministry._ And out of the Church System, with all its entrails, within which they are currently stuck.

I will talk about this later, but it needs to be stated here: I love the Church. It belongs to the Father. He loves it. He is not frustrated or disappointed with it. He is still present and working within it. Christ died for it. So, none of what follows is intended to criticize, hurt, or harm. It is simply observations and things learned from the trenches, most of them quite positive, from all these years in Kingdom living and Kingdom business.

Aside from this **Introduction** this book is broken into three parts.

Part One is an exposition on the current condition of the Church, which lends itself to the need for small group ministry of any type to grow strong in the West, in 2024 and beyond. This is coupled with a biblical definition and explanation of just what ministry, or "Church," or the phrase "from house to house" is intended to look like in the twenty-first century.

Part Two challenges the reader to come into alignment with the Kingdom of God and then defines in full detail house churches in general and Home Gatherings specifically. Herein is also discovered the amazing connection between the Kingdom and this style of ministry.

Part Three brings the practices of small group ministry, or Home Gatherings, to the table; the what's, the when's, the how's, and the why's therein. There are many questions to be asked regarding this style of ministry and this Part offers my answers, from the trenches, to at least most of those inquiries.

Please note: I use the word *man* in two different manners. There are times when I use it as man, the male species, and there are also times when I use it as man, humankind, which includes men, women, and children. I am not differentiating in the text, but the context should make it clear.

In concluding this Introduction, I believe it is imperative to recognize that regardless of one's theological positions or traditions, there are two realities going on around us at this time that need to be identified, acknowledged, and embraced.

One is that Holy Spirit, with his presence and power, has been present and accounted for since the beginning and up to and including today. And will be tomorrow. We do well to not underestimate that statement. He is the same yesterday and today and forever, and is more than willing and more than capable of being Lord in any and all situations and circumstances. (Hebrews 13:8) We do well to give him that. We do well to yield to that.

The other is that regarding this style of ministry, there is a full-on move of Holy Spirit manifesting in our midst that will only increase at this time, for a time. The more we are willing and able to see, welcome, and embrace this truth, the more we will connect with and be used by him in this current move. We do well to embrace the realization that we have entered into a significant increase in anointing in the area of this type and style of ministry. I pray for you there more than in any other area of your life. Enter in!

PART ONE

An Exposition on the Current State of Affairs within the Church at Large

---

CHAPTER ONE

SALLY AND ANNIE

A s it stands in 2024, the Church at large continues to be in a very challenging state and condition. I believe this to be primarily a leadership issue. This is not to slam or discount leaders at any level. I too am a leader, and face daily the struggles and challenges with other leaders and our followers. I am not trying to offer up a labor/management argument. It is too simplistic to offer a broad stroke statement aimed at leadership as the issue, when it is more complex than that. Yet, at the end of the day the buck does stop there.

It has been said, "As goes the husband/father, so goes the family." The same is true within the church (local) and the Church (at large). As goes the pastor/leader, man or woman, so goes the fellowship/ organization. Whether it be the head of a family, a local church, or the head of an international denomination or ministry, _leaders need to lead_. And the manner in which they do so has a direct effect on their followers, and all the people in their circle of influence. I realize that for the most part I am preaching to the choir. And yet sometimes the choir needs to hear…

I was in a post-graduate class awhile back entitled, "Leadership in the Church." The professor was a seasoned senior leader at a local church and operating in an adjunct position. Most of the students were fairly young, having just graduated from an under-graduate program of some sort, and were eager to learn and get on with what they would classify as their ministry. She took this as a prime opportunity and structured her curriculum accordingly. The syllabus went something like this: Read these five books written by current quality leaders in the American Church, write these three papers, answer these twenty-five questions. When you are done, you will have formulated your methodology, your leadership model, for your career in leading your church. Sound familiar?

That's all wonderful, except for one little thing. Not a single lick of that was biblical. She was totally missing the point. And much to my chagrin, misleading another handful of young, impressionable students down a path that was sure to cause them much difficulty at some point in their future. I gently approached her after our first class and asked her a few questions. What about the clear scriptural principle that speaks to the lordship of Christ in our lives? The principle that says he is God and we are not? The truth that tells us to follow his lead? Shouldn't we be spending our time learning how to better hear his voice so we can better align with these well-defined principles? Shouldn't we be learning how to better follow his lead, so we can help others to do the same? Are we going to spend any time going there?

She looked at me like she was a deer and I was the headlights on a car. She had no tangible idea what I was talking about. And she had no intention of considering what I was talking about. And there we were. And here we are. To her, leadership had all to do with the practics of directing others toward whatever she thought they should be moving toward. Okay. But that is not at all God's definition…

Many church and ministry leaders in this country are either burned out, are on the doorstep of being burned out, or are actually past being burned out and are full-on into exist/survival mode. They eat and breathe hope deferred. Consequently, on one level or another, they have mostly just checked out. And this ad nauseum. I am so burdened for all of this. I have seen too much of the negative, and this often in the midst of what could fairly easily be turned about to the wonderful positives that our Lord and Savior so desires…

This book is about house churches. We call them Home Gatherings, but more on that later. It's about small groups, about effective and life-giving leadership and ministry in that context. But it is also about helping people, good, even great people, who are stuck in a system they did not create. They just got stuck in it somewhere along the way. And now they don't know what they are, where they are, and most of all, who they are. This grieves me so much; I am crying as I write this. I get it because I've been through it. I thought this was the right way. I was taught this was the right way. This is why I am so burdened. There are answers. From Scripture, from the Teacher, the Counselor. There are solutions. And yet, the problem not only remains but seems to continue to worsen.

Let's change that.
Let's figure out how to get much closer to the Creator of it all and align with him as he changes that.

To continue our personal story from the Introduction, we moved on in our journey from the singles group to a church plant. Within that plant we built small groups. We were meeting weekly in our home with a group of folks, most of whom were a part of our church. We had been meeting for six months or so, when one evening, during a time of what we call prayer ministry, one of the women, we'll call her Sally, opened up about her strained relationship with heavenly Father. She shared, through many tears, the anguish and heartache she was feeling as she was trying to walk a close walk with God, but had much by way of hope deferred and faith dashed. She admitted to being angry with God over several things that had happened, and some that had not happened, the net result of which had produced an emptiness in her heart and a distance from her Lord. She was honest about this and was seeking help and prayer.

Sally was able to open up about something that was deep in her heart for one reason: she was in an arena of trust. We are very intentional, very emphatic, about building that arena in all encounters we have with others. I grew up in an environment of significant mistrust, though I didn't know that at the time. It was not until years later, after giving my life to Jesus, that he pulled this reality from the depths of my heart and put it on the table for examination and surgery. The result of that healing was that I came to a much stronger and deeper understanding of trust, and the One called Trust. It is imperative. Healings, on all levels; transformations of the heart and mind; deliverances, from things natural or supernatural, do not readily happen except in an environment of trust.

Ultimately, it is God and God alone who is trust and who brings trust into the mix. Jesus is also trust in that he exercises trust; he builds and gives trust. It is an action. It becomes an action within us when we embrace and grow in it. As we follow him, as we learn to live by his example, we come to trust him; we come to be highly impacted by the fact that he is not only trust but he does trust. Thus, we must learn to trust and give it away – as it has been given to us.

One of the other women in the group jumped in and suggested what we were dealing with here was a demon of rebellion against God, against authority – and we needed to cast it out now before it gained more of a hold in her life. As the leader of the group, and ever the teacher, I had the responsibility to direct the flow of our time, ideally with the mind of the Lord operating in and through me. The Lord had revealed to me from the beginning of Sally's dialog what was behind her pain.

After thanking her for being brave enough to be that transparent, and after thanking the other woman for her input into the situation, and acknowledging that sometimes demons do attack, thus affirming her, I suggested to all that what was really going on here was not a demonic inroad or manifestation. Rather, it was a sincere, devout child/woman of God crying out for more of God. I offered that we could pray over her and ask that the love of the Father enter into our midst and touch her heart greatly. We did.

She was absolutely overwhelmed by the love and the presence of God, the Father, Daddy. (Jesus refers to his Heavenly Father as "Abba". That word translates fully into English as "Daddy." (Mark 14:36; see also Romans 8:15, Galatians 4:6)) He settled on her and ministered to her heart in an intimate way that only he and she could know. He brought healing to her heart as he showed her over and over his love for her, his care for her, his heart for her - and her value to him. Sally walked away a different woman that night. Life, overall and with her Lord and King, gained much that evening and she went on in a much sweeter, stronger, healthier way. Sally had hope restored and renewed through the workings of Father God.

To further explain and clarify: The love of the Father is ever present. If one is born-again, then the love of the Father is ever present in their heart. I have learned that he flows in levels and degrees of depth and intensity, sometimes manifesting elements of his character more than at other times. He does this for the purpose of expressing and exercising his love for his creation. This is what happened to Sally that evening.

I offer that story to illustrate a point Father God has so graciously -- and vehemently -- worked into my heart. We all need each other. We all need strong and healthy relationships. We are created for just that, with the Lord and with each other. Sally had been carrying that hurt and pain for some time. Father knew all about it. In his timing, he could have touched her at any point in time and brought healing to her heart. He can do that. He is sovereign. But in the workings of his Kingdom, he most often chooses a different way.

This is so critical to see, understand, and exercise:

**God chooses to minister _to_ his people
through his people. All of his people.
And this regardless of where we think we
are or aren't in and with him.
It is never about us!**

He is sovereign. He can bring the supernatural
realm in our lives at will. But see this:

**Because his heart is for us and he desires
to be with us in our world,
most often he chooses to meet us on our level,
and thus to exhaust the natural before
offering the supernatural.**

Most often he uses situations and circumstances, people and relationships to work in us, to answer prayer, so as to exercise his sovereignty. This truth is critical in the building of house churches, in the building of any ministry gig that is intending to seek and reflect the Kingdom of God. We must come to understand, flow, and live in his plan, his agenda.

Don't misunderstand me. I am a strong believer in the supernatural. God is Spirit and he is spiritual. He loves manifesting himself in our lives. The work of Holy Spirit abounds. But in the midst of his workings, he wants us to work with him, to be vessels through whom he can operate. It is simply part of his economy, his Kingdom principles. It is simply part of his love for his creation. Sally got totally blasted by the Spirit of God. He used those around her to deliver that blast. That truth is powerful, and it is very fulfilling for all parties involved.

That truth only happens via relationship. Could the Father have sent the Spirit to minister to Sally in a dream or in her personal prayer time? Yes. Does that sort of thing happen? Often. Could he have healed her heart through a stranger in the mall or on a street corner? Yes. Does that ever happen? Yes, it does. But mostly not. Why? Because, again, he wants to bless; because he wants to be in the middle of our lives, individually and collectively. He wants to partner with us, flow in and through us, and use us. He wants relationship with us, and he wants us to have relationship with each other. For his glory and our maturity. For his glory and our growth. For his glory and our gain.

Let's consider the ramifications of this element of God's heart within another story. A good friend of ours, let's call her Annie, said once, "I will never be in another one of your small groups." What was behind that statement? I'm not being critical, but she was not willing to let Holy Spirit go deep. At that time, she was not willing to allow those whom she trusted the most to be used by Holy Spirit to bring out the wounds and the resultant pain for the purposes of healing. She had multiple inner issues, not the least of which was an inability to allow trust to grow and develop between her and God and between her and other people. Contrast this to the story about Sally, who was able and willing, again, within the arena of trust, to open her heart to her Lord; and who then received healing in that area of her life.

Annie had, from her vantage point, too much pain, too much hurt, to allow herself to experience the kind of ministry Sally received. This is totally understandable and is not to be criticized, judged, or put down in any manner. Holy Spirit is patient and kind. Because he loves us so very much, he is also ruthless! He will continue to work on the inner-man issues, on the mistrust that is present for obvious reasons. But know this: He will not stop until he has it all! All the pain, all the woundedness, all the trouble and torment of the soul, all the sin that has come as a result of being sinned against, all the hiding and escaping that is exercised to avoid all the other things identified in this paragraph. Again, because of his great love for his creation, all of these things will be healed and/or removed by the time he is done.

This is one of the primary reasons why small group ministry is so important to our God. If you catch nothing else from this book, catch this: We are all important to him. We are all valuable to him. He wishes to demonstrate his love by working and living with and through us to that place of completion, of wholeness.

Here is the point of these stories, of this chapter: The Church was never intended to be about some human propagating their ideas and passions while everyone else sits by. That is not God. His ways are all-inclusive. Everybody has a part. Everybody has a job, a role, a responsibility in his Kingdom. And when we can finally agree with that, and adjust who we are to that, life takes on a whole different depth, a whole different value, and a whole different meaning.

You know, when he hung on that cross for you, for your life, he redeemed you. To redeem is to purchase. When I last went to the grocery store and bought that loaf of bread, I redeemed it. Okay, so see this: When he redeemed you, he redeemed all of you, the good, the bad, and the ugly. He redeemed your heart, your soul, your body. He also redeemed all of your stuff, your junk, your baggage, or whatever words you choose to label them. Now it all belongs to him, and what he chooses to do with it is entirely up to him. Rest assured that when he is done with you there will be no stuff, junk or baggage remaining. Ponder that...

CHAPTER TWO

ANTICIPATE THE
LORD'S MOVING

A number of years back I received a prophetic word from the Lord. He prompted me about a portion of an interview I had seen with Wayne Gretsky, perhaps one of the best men to ever play the game of professional hockey. Upon being asked, "What makes you so good?" he replied in an honest and humble manner. He said, and I am paraphrasing, "If that is true, it is because most players go to where the puck is. I go to where it is going." In other words, he was able to anticipate the play well enough to be ahead of it, connect with the puck, and either score or assist on a score.

The Lord then said to me, "Go where I am going. There is nothing wrong with where I am, I am there. But go where I am going." It seemed to me that the next most logical thing was to simply ask, "Okay, where are you going?!" (Don't you just love the way the Lord sometimes sets us up?) To which he answered, "I am going into the living and dining and family rooms; I am going into the small groups, into the house churches in America."

That was a long time ago. That word came to me shortly after we had moved across the country - to where we have lived since, and to a whole different level of ministry. It was a prophetic word for the Church. It was also a word and an invitation for us personally. I believe, concerning the Church at large, that that word is more apropos and applicable today than it was twenty-plus years ago! In this man's opinion, the West in general, and specifically America, has not been ready for the varieties of small group ministry models seen in certain other countries. That does not have to be a negative statement. It was true. But now, what America is ready for is culturally relevant, scripturally accurate, life inducing small groups, however they might be labeled. He has clearly stated he is already there, waiting for us to show up!

> **"Every time God has offered, we have taken**
> **much less than what he was willing to give.**
> **It is time to take [the fullness] of what he is**
> **offering, of what he wants to give."**[1]
> (Brackets mine)

In the midst of learning how to anticipate the Lord, and follow him accordingly, it is imperative that this pursuit be of and by Holy Spirit. That is to say it must be Spirit-filled, Spirit-led, and then Spirit-directed. (Here are some of the Scriptures that support this statement: Spirit-filled: Luke 1:15, 4:1; Acts 2:4, 4:8, 4:31, 7:55, 11:24, 13:19, 13:52. Spirit-led: Luke 12:12; John 14:26; 1 Corinthians 2:13; Acts 10:19-20, 13:2, 16:16; Romans 8:14; Galatians 5:18, 5:25.)

These Scriptures give evidence and proof of the Spirit's involvement in the lordship of Christ. Prayer and intercession, worship, prayer ministry, signs and wonders, power encounters, healings, deliverances, all the gifts of the Spirit, deep and significant heart and life changes, all authored and secured by the Spirit. All this is essential. And, again, all this is available today under his lordship.

Primary here is the reality of the relationship, mentioned in the Introduction, and its results. For example, it is fact that in our part of the planet eighty-five percent of all people who say yes to Jesus come to him via a personal relationship, a friend.[2] People saying yes to Jesus mostly come as a result of a person in relationship with the Lord, through whom Holy Spirit flows, awakening their hearts. This is our Lord ministering to his people through his people. Healings, physical, mental and spiritual, come in that same manner: as a result of a life dedicated to Jesus, through whom Holy Spirit flows, into the life of another. Peace, joy, all the fruits of the Spirit (Galatians 5:22-23) come in the midst of deep relationship with Jesus, within which is found the Spirit of Jesus, Holy Spirit. (Act 16:7) I am being redundant to drive a point.

This is how we are called to function within the Church, which is within _his_ Church, which is actually within _his_ Kingdom. The challenge is that as biblical as all of this is, it is most often not taught. And so, it is not known or sought after. We must learn to anticipate the Lord and follow his lead.

The issue is that the Church system, in its current condition, is broken. Broken in so many ways, in so many pieces, that many, perhaps even most, do not know it is broken. It is the king with no clothes on.[3] It is the frog in the kettle, with the frog having no clue or indication that the temperature is rising and it is being boiled for dinner.[4] Throw a frog in a pot of hot water and he will jump right out. Put him in a pot of tepid, lukewarm water (See Revelation 3:15-16) and then turn up the heat and he will sit there until he is dinner. He cannot, he does not, notice the subtle changes, and thus he is cooked.

Many of the troublesome characteristics of what we all call church are so engrained, having been a part of the mix for so long they are not even noticed or recognized. Many of these aspects are traditions. In and of themselves, traditions are not wrong. But when they take on a higher place, a higher point of value than they should, when they become the standard, they cause trouble. And we are cooked.

I am reminded of the story of the mom who decided to teach her daughter how to cook a ham. One afternoon they set out to do so. Mom had already purchased the ham. She set it on the counter and proceeded to cut a few inches off one of the ends. Before she got to the next step her daughter asked, "Wait. What? Why did you just do that?" Her mom thought for a moment and replied, "Well, that is how your grandmother taught me." "Okay." said the daughter, "But why?" "Well, now that you mention it, I guess I don't know for sure. Let's call her and ask."

So, they called Grandma and asked her. Her response was epic! "Oh honey. I only did that so that the ham would fit into that particular pan!" And her daughter had been doing that ever since – with different pans that had different dimensions. It took the inquisitiveness of the granddaughter to capture and expose what had become a tradition; one without any merit except in the moment all those years ago. An action that morphed into a tradition, and wasted a lot of ham! And, again, we are cooked.

This story is very reflective of much of what we experience in today's Church environments. Much of what is done has no real and tangible bearing on today, on the felt needs of all the people, or on the heart and intentions of God for his people. In Genesis, the cloud and the pillar of fire were dynamic; they kept moving because the Lord was moving. It is no different today; he is always moving. And yet these things of man remain mostly static. Eight words that comprise some of the saddest words in the Church and in Church history: "We have never done it that way before." And this with the clear implication that we won't be doing it that way now either.

A quote from Charles Spurgeon, in the context of yielding to God, of letting God be God, is apropos here:

> "Observe how sovereign the operations of God are… He may in one district work a revival, and persons may be stricken down, and made to cry aloud, [or express some other manifestation] but in another place there may be crowds, and yet all may be still and quiet, as though no deep excitement [which was his word for tangible Holy Spirit activity] existed at all… He *can* bless as he wills and he *will* bless as he wills. **Let us not dictate to God.** Many a blessing has been lost by Christians not believing it to be a blessing, because it did not come in the particular

shape which they had conceived to be proper and right."[5] (Emphasis and brackets mine)

I was invited into a church one time to consult with leadership. Over time, things for them had gone downhill, gotten a bit better, and then gotten much worse. This was a church with a history of being in the charismatic/Spirit-led camp. Leadership had shifted, struggles and conflict had developed and that is when I received invitation. Within the conversations regarding their Sunday service the senior leader made a very revealing statement, "Holy Spirit can do anything he wants. He just has 45 minutes to do it in." And there it is: His tradition, and thus his leadership, had little to do with God's heart and his leadership. And, one more time, we are cooked.

The biggest problem in these scenarios is that these traditions, these methodologies, that are at the heart of this broken system, by and large, are not biblical. Some of them are not even close. They are mostly concocted by the minds and hearts of man, for the purposes and gain of man. The discussion on this topic is beyond tired. For the better part of my life in ministry, which is now on the far edge of forty years, this discussion has been going on, and there is evidence to suggest it has seemingly been going on for literally centuries. Probably most of it has been in the wrong places and with the wrong people.

From Wolfgang Simson in his book, *The House Church Book*,

> "The image of much of contemporary Christianity could be described as holy people coming regularly to a holy place on a holy day at a holy hour to participate in a holy ritual led by a holy man dressed in holy clothes for a holy fee. Since this regular performance-oriented enterprise, called a 'worship service,' requires a lot of organizational talent and administrative bureaucracy, formalized and institutionalized patterns develop quickly into

rigid traditions. Statistically, a traditional one- or two-hour worship service is very resource-hungry but produces very little fruit in terms of discipling people and changing lives. Economically, it is a high-input, low-output structure. Traditionally, the desire to worship 'in the right way' has led to denominationalism, confessionalism, and nominalism. This ignores the fact that Christians are called to worship 'in spirit and in truth' rather than in cathedrals holding songbooks. It also ignores the fact that most of life is informal; and so, too, is Christianity, as [it is] 'the Way of Life.' We need to change from being powerful actors to people who act powerfully."[6] (Brackets mine)

I think Tozer captured it best when he said,

"A spiritual kingdom lies all around us, enclosing us, embracing us, altogether within reach of our inner selves, waiting for us to recognize it [waiting for us to engage it – and its author]. God himself is here waiting our response to his presence. This eternal world will come alive to us [in ever greater dimension] the moment we reckon upon its reality."[8] (Brackets mine)

There is a serious and significant need to get past the current place of living and step into this reality. A need for us to get past self and our creature comforts; to see and get past all the self-orientation, the self-sins. They would be the sins of self-righteousness, self-confidence, self-sufficiency, self-admiration, self-pity, and self-love. In and of themselves, some of these expressions of self can be balanced within a right relationship with our Lord. But mostly they are over played, overly focused on, and actually keeping us from what he wants with us.

There is a need to see the value in a lifestyle, a community of believers, wherein Jesus is Lord — and we are not. Can we simply follow his lead and allow him to change us into men and women of God that are all in for him, his Kingdom, and his way? Can we then enter into that sweet, wonderful, and intended place of a continual anticipation of the Lord's presence and power?

In his book *Ekklesia*, Ed Silvoso asks a number of key questions that are quite pertinent to our discussions and pursuits:

> "How was the New Testament Church able not just to survive, but also to radically transform the hostile social and political environs into which it was born? How did it set in motion a process that impacted nations in a relatively short time, *without buildings, professional clergy, religious freedom or social status*? Why, in comparison, does it appear that the Church's influence on social matters today is progressively diminishing? Could it be that in our generation the fullness of the *real* Jesus has yet to be discovered, as well as the actual depth of our call as ministers? Could it be that we have confined to four walls once a week what is designed to be a 24/7 people movement out in the marketplace, transforming our cities and nations? And could it be that we have restricted ministry to professionally trained specialists, instead of ministry being the work of all the saints?"[7]

He goes on, in the context of small group type ministry, to offer some powerful answers.

There is another way. As was previously stated, we must learn to anticipate the Lord and follow his lead. We must learn to listen for his voice – and respond accordingly. He is fully invested in us, in our lives. We must ask him to help us to learn how to pursue him in this same manner. There are options. His. There are solutions. His.

DR. JAY SLIFE

CHAPTER THREE

SOLUTION ONE: SUBMIT TO THE LORDSHIP OF JESUS

There is another way. It is imperative that we learn how to anticipate the Lord and follow his lead. It is also imperative that we learn to not only listen for his voice but also to respond accordingly. The truth is that he is fully invested in us. So, one more time, it is imperative that we seek him for the help we need to learn how to pursue him in the same manner. There really are options. And there really are solutions. From his heart to ours. Can we go there?

These next four chapters offer four different solutions that blend and work together. To me, they set the table for all of life. They also set the table for Part Two and Three, which are comprised of the practics of this type of ministry. I am not the answer man; I don't pretend to be. That position has been taken by Holy Spirit. What I am offering, based on my years of experience, are what I believe to be the main points of importance, that I have gleaned from him.

A very good friend of mine, let's call him Sam, spent a number of years traveling the country operating as a highly anointed servant of God. He was functioning in the realm of an apostolic/prophetic ministry, bringing counsel and consultation to church leaders; be it church-wide, denomination-wide, or network-wide. On one particular occasion he had been invited in to spend several days with a senior pastor, let's call him Joe, his staff and lay leaders, and the body at large. Sound familiar? One afternoon Sam and Joe were talking strategy. Joe brought up the currently defunct Men's

Ministry and offered an idea. He wanted to have a Men's Pancake Breakfast as a means of re-launching the group. He was looking for Sam's input. Sam wisely suggested that:

The best strategy would be to spend some concerted time with the Lord – the Chief Strategist - and hear from him just what to do and how to proceed.

Joe's response was classic – and reveals what I believe is one of the primary underlying issues in most any and all ministry attempts or endeavors, small or large, local or trans local. He said, "Yeah, yeah. But what about the pancake breakfast?" Deep sigh. Joe was not at all interested in hearing what God had to say about Joe's ministry. He had no concept or belief system that put God at the head of God's church. Joe was the head of his church, and in that he was running a church that looked and acted much more like CEO Christianity than Jesus-is-Lord Christianity. Still sound familiar? We must come to the lordship of Christ in who we are, and from there in what we do.

We cannot assume, and create serious trouble if we do, that just because we are walking with him in the realm of leadership that our will is his will.

Jesus is Lord. His lordship makes him Leader or Master. That makes us servants, or bond-servants, or slaves, depending on the translation you read. Please recognize that the word "slave" here has nothing to do with the negativity associated with that word in our country. In this context, in the economy of God's Kingdom, God's lordship is not a political or societal word. It is a relational word that brings nothing negative to the table. Except the loss of our flesh, our self, which when the fruit of that is seen is no loss at all.

Let me use a different word, which can help to bring a different understanding. The first solution is to yield, to submit. It is to actually, practically, and tangibly come to the place in life where the lordship of the Christ is where we live. Not just partially, but completely. And not just with lip service or intellectual understanding, but within the brokenness brought by God. The result of this brokenness yields us to his lordship, to the *joy* found in his lordship, to the *peace* and *fulfillment* found in his lordship in our lives. Allowing him to lead and guide us from his place as Lord puts the responsibility, the weight on him. It allows him his way – and brings great *freedom* to us. Thus, the joy, peace, and fulfillment. Perhaps this is best understood from Scripture.

Psalm 51:17 says, "The sacrifices of God are a broken spirit; a broken and contrite heart, O God, you will not despise." That is a reasonable translation, but the Septuagint is closer to the original text and says it much better: "A sacrifice to God is a spirit being broken. God will not treat with contempt a heart being broken and humbled."

Researching into the words in this passage brings further light to the text. The passage could be written this way: "Yielding, giving away my attitudes, agendas, and actions to God, to the One having much more value than I, is allowing my inner-man to be continually broken into pieces; thus, putting me in a position of subservience to him, in all aspects of my being. I am found entirely worthy by God when I submit to this process; to the process of allowing him to break, and subsequently rebuild, both my mind and spirit." (Paraphrase mine)

I want this. I want to be found entirely worthy by God. How about you?

This lordship business is not at all easy. Barna's research says that only nine percent of born-again Christians actually live in the place where Christ is first, in this place of lordship. That means ninety-one percent of born-again believers in this country use the standards of this world to make life decisions, to direct their paths.[1]

My research, albeit much more limited than Barna's, would suggest that that percentage is more like three or four percent.

It is not easy. However, his grace is sufficient for me in that process, and for you too. "I believe a life with Jesus is designed and intended to bring us to ever deeper places in him relationally. I believe we have been created for just this. There are probably an infinite number of truths (John 14:6) coming from his heart, which he works into us over the course of a life with him, on this side and the other. To me, at this point in my life, there are three that stand out above the rest. There are three things he will work into my soul, my mind and spirit, that he will have me living in and living out: patience, humility, and his glory. I also believe that the first two being worked simultaneously will reveal the third. It does not work in any other order."[2]

If God is truly in control, is truly our Lord, then we owe it to him to let him have that control. We owe it to him to let him lead. We owe it to him to learn to listen, hear his voice, and follow. Lordship has all to do with the one who is lord. In this case, it is the one who is Lord. He leads, we follow. By his Spirit we need to get our direction, our instruction. By his Spirit we need to get our marching orders. We may "plan our course," but if we are wise, we allow "the Lord to determine our steps." This happens when we, "Commit to the Lord whatever you do, and your plans will succeed." (Proverbs 16:9 and 16:3)

We tend to not follow Jesus as much as we follow others. We tend to follow the person who led us to Christ in the first place. Or we tend to follow after a particular leader, or someone we admire. We have been taught, it has been modeled for us, to operate mostly in our own strength and understanding. We decide what we are going to do – and then ask God to bless it. And because he loves us, he often does. But that is not the biblical way. That ends up being the good that is not the best. The best is to follow his lead and distinctly not ask him to follow ours. The best is to yield and pattern our lives after the One who came to be our example.

　　　　　　　DR. JAY SLIFE

That is the call. And when we finally agree to allow him the right to work that yieldedness and submission into our soul, our spirit, we then are fully surrendered to his plans and purposes. And from there whatever he chooses to do in us, with us, and through us will be his way. This brings a full freedom to us, an amazing sense of fulfillment in us, and glory to his name.

Coming now into a new season, a new and fresh outpouring of our Lord, it behooves us to allow him to change us. Let's go there.

From the beginning, he created us for relationship, as sons and daughters. That makes him Father, and we are to follow his lead. Does the clay say to potter, "Why have you made me so, and just what are you doing to me anyway?" (Isaiah 64:8, paraphrase mine) It is called lordship. He leads, we follow. But we, the larger body of followers of Jesus, mostly don't live there. Quite often we don't even know to live there; we have not been taught or instructed in that way. We tend to ask him to bless whatever it is that we want to do, or be, that we think is the best plan for us. We may even base that asking or that plan on strong moral and biblical principles. Again, he loves us and often does bless us. And, again, that most often settles into the good that is not the best. And sometimes it results in unnecessary struggle and difficulty, in frustration and hope deferred. I don't know about you, but I want what is best, and I am willing to sacrifice the good to get it. I am willing to sacrifice my will, my want, for his.

I worked with a gentleman once in helping him develop his business. To his advantage, he had many tools in his toolbox. He was sharp, witty, personable, reasonably knowledgeable, and had enough energy for the both of us. He was well on his way to cultivating a successful business, at least one that was successful in his eyes. One of his underlying ideologies was that of living his life, including his business, with "Jesus as my co-pilot." That is a noble idea, and one that is common in Christian circles. The challenge is that as noble as it is, it is not at all biblical.

God is never the co-pilot or co-partner, not by his decrees, his imperatives. Do we partner with him? Yes, but in that context, he is clearly the senior partner and we are definitively and by far his junior.

Lordship is difficult. It requires a yielding, a submitting of my will to the will of my Lord and King. Jesus said, "Come, follow me, and I will make you fishers of men." (Matthew 9:9) We can all get behind that with excitement and determination. But he also said, "If anyone would come after me, he must deny himself and take up his cross and follow me." (Matthew 16:24)

This is where it becomes more difficult. Lordship not only calls for, it also requires and demands the denying of self, the taking up of one's cross, and the following of someone else's lead, in this case that of the Father. There rests the tension point that is as old as humanity, as old as Adam and Eve, as Cain and Abel – and as current as you and me. Following does not come naturally, especially following all the way to lordship. It is a learned behavior. It is an acquired taste. The usual pattern is that we follow as long as it suits us, as long as we can still be in some semblance of control with our plans and agendas.

Jesus wanted his own way, too. In Matthew 26:39 (NASB) he said, "My Father, if it is possible, let this cup pass from me…" He is expressing his own desire, his own will. He does not want to drink that cup. But he goes on. In the same breath he says, "…yet not as I will, but as you will." The KJV says, "…nevertheless not as I will, but as thou wilt."

It is in the *nevertheless* that the battle for lordship is fought, and either won or lost.

Is it really that simple? I believe it to be so. It is also quite complex. That is because we want it our way. Therein lies the rub. We humans tend to complicate things, to muddy the water with our pride, our rebellion, and our independence. We tend to make things more difficult with our need to inject our own perspectives, intentions, and agendas. We resist the lordship of the Father because we want management and control of our own lives. Honestly, in our natural ways, we don't want to yield or submit to anyone, least of all to God. We yield, but mostly only to the point where we still maintain some aspect of control.

If we are steeped in religion, in "formulated Christianity," seeking formulas to embrace, to attach ourselves to, then we are stuck right there. Our god is then our formula. The Christian world, the religious world, is full of this. It is the way of humanity. Religion, clearly defined, has nothing to do with some spiritual dynamic. That is just where it fits so well, by the hand of man. Religion is best defined as, "a set of rules and parameters bringing a specific order of control."[3] In this context then, it is quite easy to reduce the Word, the Lord, the Spirit to a formula. This reduces Jesus from a relationship, from a relational God, to a system, to a systematic god. We are all genuinely in dire need of a Savior – and a Lord. We have to see the challenge as it has been for untold centuries and change it -- by coming to the fullness of lordship.

Jesus put it this way: "I tell you the truth, the Son can do nothing by himself; He can do only what he sees his Father doing, because whatever the Father does the Son also does. By myself I can do nothing ...for I seek not to please myself but him who sent me." (John 5:19, 30) He is exercising his will by submitting it to the Father. He is using words such as "nothing" and "only" and "whatever," which speak to his emphatic choice to yield to his Father's lordship.

Philippians 2:5-8 says, "Your attitude [and resultant purpose and behavior] should be the same as that of Christ Jesus who ...made himself nothing, ...humbled himself and became obedient [to the Father,] to death, even death on a cross!" (Brackets mine) If we are not intentionally living there, we are missing the mark. He is always to be our example.

A long time ago, as in back to Constantine and the melding of the Church into the then-current socio-political-economic system commonly referred to as government, the Church became systematized and sunk into a predominantly man-made, man-centered entity. The Protestant Reformation did much but it did not change this issue, as the Church was still not focused upon the lordship of Christ. And this now to the place where much or even most of today's Church has no comprehension or expression of lordship. Instead, it is patterned almost entirely after a secular corporate model of doing business, with an application of that model focused on numerical growth by way of entertainment. Some have called it CEO Christianity. Not that there is anything inherently wrong with the corporate business model so common amongst us. But it is distinctly not a biblical model.[4] Others have gone so far as to call this current condition the, "black hole of Christianity."[5]

The New Testament model of ministry does not support the system the Church has created, and even coveted, for centuries. Within the biblical model it is not about a man, a point-person, per se. It is not about a system that for the most part removes the essence of God's workings from the many, and instead puts very high expectations on the few professionals, many of whom are unfortunately under-trained and ill-equipped for the job. Rather, it is about hands-on ministry for all, following the lead of the Lord Jesus and his Father.

The New Testament model dovetails perfectly into the world of twenty-first century living, if it is properly aligned. It truly is all hands on deck. Everyone has a place, a purpose, a role, and a function. Everyone has an assignment, a directive. Everyone has value! This model produces fruit, the kind of fruit that has the texture, taste, and aroma of the Father. This model recognizes that *we are all called to full-time ministry*, no matter our place, level of education, or genetics. Everybody is employed. It has nothing to do with place or position. It has nothing to do with vocation. It has all to do with following the lead of the Lord.

DR. JAY SLIFE

The model demonstrated by Peter and his friends as fishermen in the Gospels, Paul as a tentmaker in Acts and beyond, and untold others following their lead, is the model we must develop and fully support. This model of lordship puts God as the head and allows for him to flow through his established parameters and formats found in Scripture to train and equip all for his works of service. (Ephesians 4:12-13) This model is centered around him and none other.

Within the context of the lordship of Christ, I believe there is a spiritual dynamic often missing in the understandings and discussions of many with regards to spiritual instruction and growth, including spiritual warfare. What is missing is the leading of Holy Spirit that brings *revelation*. Our wisdoms and insights, as good as they may be, are simply not enough. Without his lordship we are stuck and going in circles. When we work to build or accomplish in our own intellect, strengths, and understandings, without the acknowledgment of, and full engagement with, the Spirit, we miss it. We miss the strategies for action, the strategies for warfare, the directions, and the course corrections. We miss the covering and the critical elements required for success, for completion of whatever the project or pursuit may be. The whole argument regarding Church growth and development needing to come from a biblical base is worthless – unless it is predicated on this reality. The efforts of man without the lordship of Christ are futile. "Unless the Lord builds the house, its builders labor in vain." (Psalm 127:1)

On the other hand, the upside of this truth is powerful. If we will but yield, if we will but submit to his lordship, at all costs - and the cost is very high - if we will but be still, listen and respond to the lead of the Spirit, in all things and at all times, we cannot fail! Has God ever failed?

What I am saying is that often we don't even think to let God lead. Mostly our modus operandi is to create something and ask him to bless it as we go. Therein lies the dilemma. We must be careful; we must be more careful, perhaps more intentional when considering just exactly what God is saying, and in just exactly how we are going to receive, understand, and apply it to the task at hand. Transformation does not come through a missed application of the truth. It will come by way of the full and complete truth applied, which is found in relationship and then in lordship.

We must come to the place where we "live and move and have our being" (Acts 17:28) within the heart and lifeblood of Matthew 6:33, which says, "…seek first his Kingdom and his righteousness, and all these things will be given to you as well." This passage is paramount to all who would align with God as he continues to pour out his heart for his people around the earth. Especially in the days in which we live. We have already established the need and value in lordship. This passage is the anchor for that truth.

The immediate context of this passage, verses 25 to 34, which is found within the larger context of what has been labeled the Sermon on the Mount, has Jesus talking about worry and anxiety over the things of life. He says in verse 25, "…do not worry about your life…" He goes on to list a number of other things not to worry about; things such as food, clothing, and provision therein. He points out that the pagans "run after all these things" and thus have their focus there. He then says that, "…your heavenly Father knows that you have need of them" (KJV) In light of that, in light of the Father knowing we have needs, comes our verse.

Paraphrased it could read this way, "In light of your needs, and the Father's awareness of them, seek first, pay attention first, focus on and pursue first the King within his Kingdom. Then his righteousness, which is his manner of right-living, and all of the things that you need and concern over will be taken care of, will be given to you." This is lordship. This is the Kingdom. Our part is to prioritize all that we are, and all that we do, such that the King is considered first, from which we make the conscious choice to yield, submit, and obey his directives.

My primary mentor from years gone by once told this story. At one point, he was the point person within a ministry set up by an international organization. He was traveling all over the country and the world helping leaders lead, helping churches large and small grow to the next level. He was doing a great job, or so it seemed. Eventually, however, because much of his great work was coming from within his own strength and energy – and not from his God, he became totally exhausted and was becoming burned out. Late one night he was sitting in an airport waiting for his flight home - and complaining to the Lord about his current situation. In the midst of his gripe session with Jesus, the Lord said this to Him: "I have seen your ministry. And quite frankly, I'm not impressed. *Why don't you let me show you mine?*"[6] (Emphasis mine) Ouch. This man was an amazing teacher, with an amazing insight into Scripture, and with an amazing ability to discern, understand, and apply the Word to life. It was how he got to where he was. He was very biblically based. But apparently, his relationship with Jesus was not yet deep enough that he was lordship based. He was not fully Kingdom oriented. This encounter changed his heart and his life forever.

Lordship is not easy. To the contrary, it can be quite difficult. On the other hand, the Lord's grace for us is quite easy. It is sufficient. In parts of 2 Corinthians 12:9-10, Paul records what the Lord said to him in the midst of his struggles with yielding, with lordship. It fits for us as well. "My Grace is sufficient for you, for my power is made perfect in weakness. That is why, for Christ's sake, I delight in weakness, …in difficulties. For when I am weak, then I am strong." Truth be told, I cannot enter into the life of the lordship of my Christ, my Lord, and all of its wonderful fruits. Not in my own strength, my own doing. I live there in his presence, with his help, by his grace. It does not happen any other way. But it does happen by his way...

CHAPTER FOUR

SOLUTION TWO: ALIGN WITH HIS WORD

I n my opinion, the Word of God, particularly in the West, in the twenty-first century, is way under played. Perhaps because it "is too difficult and confusing." Perhaps because it "contradicts itself." Perhaps because people are simply too lazy or claim to be too busy to take the time and effort required to engage it. What I find interesting is that the truth of the matter is just the opposite. The more one engages, the less difficult and confusing it becomes. This results in more clarity and an increase of desire for more of the Word.

"Man does not live on bread alone, but on every word that comes from the mouth of God." (Matthew 4:4)

♫♫ "Panting, panting, searching for the water, the water, the water.
It's not so far away… it's not so mysterious.
It's not so far away… it's not so mysterious.
Just take the scroll and eat the scroll.
Gotta take the time to fellowship with the Spirit.
If I don't drink, keep drinking, I will die.
Just like the body dies without the water, I will die without fellowship with you.
So here I am, here I am." ♫♫[1]

This quote is from some spontaneous worship led by Misty Edwards. The statement, "Just take the scroll and eat the scroll" has all to do with consuming the Word of God in a one-on-one manner with Holy Spirit. It speaks to an intimacy between the living Word and us, and you.

"In the beginning was the Word, and the Word was with God, and the Word was God. He was with God in the beginning. Through him all things were made; without him nothing was made that has been made. In him was life, [and is life], and that life was the light of men. The light shines in the darkness but the darkness has not overcome it. The Word became flesh and made his dwelling among us." (John 1:1-5, 14a. Brackets mine)

The Word of God is alive! It is living!

"For the Word of God is alive and active." (Hebrews 4:12a)

From the place of having come into alignment with his lordship, the next step is to be sure that we have come into alignment with his Word. As has been stated, the Church system, as it is and has been for so many years, often does not find the basis of its modus operandi from Scripture. Usually, it finds that from the works, efforts, and traditions of man. Let's examine what the Word has to say about Church, ministry, and connecting people with God and other people. Let's follow the lead given to us in the Word. Let's get about the business of following God's heart and intentions.

We must gain our insights, understandings, theologies, and doctrines from the Scriptures and not from the objectives and perspectives of man. And certainly not from some "prophetic word" – accurate or not. We must be willing to receive direction - and even correction - and adjust to that which God has to say. This is aligning with him, with his Word.

You know, scriptural arguments are as old as dirt! Literally! I am not here to argue doctrine or theology; that is not my point. I am not here to tell you that I am right and you are not; that is also not my point. I am here to suggest that there is a different manner in which to approach God's Word. A way that gives him room to be him, that allows him the truth of who he is. Instead of taking a piece of the Word and running with it in our own direction.

I have two daughters and a son-in-law who have an alliance with a particular NLF team. I have two sons, a son-in-law, and myself, who have a very different alliance. (And I have a wife, and they have a mother, who, bless her heart, sits on the fence not wanting to offend anyone!) We are a house divided in this area. And we have fun with it. In that context, we all learned that the more we chose to argue amongst ourselves, the more set in our positions we became. Which, of course, is of no real value, and is quite counter-productive. From that, we all learned to throttle down, to honor and respect each other in this. We do sometimes offer light banter, but we do not argue, and thus offend, each other's minds or hearts. Again, we have chosen to honor and respect.

It is my hope and intention to do the same here. In this, I will offer some thoughts and observations to hopefully illuminate and clear up some struggles that are happening in the context of biblical application to life.

"For the word of God is living and active. Sharper than any double-edged sword, it penetrates even to dividing soul and spirit, joints and marrow; it judges [weighs and measures] the thoughts and attitudes of the heart." (Hebrews 4:12 NASB, brackets mine) We do well to allow it its work, without resistance, without bias, bent, or dogma.

"Your word is a lamp unto my feet and a light unto my path. (Psalm 119:105) It lights the way. And without it we are all stumbling around in the dark, guessing and groping.

The Word of God is the standard, the plumbline, from which all else is measured. (2 Kings 21:13; Isaiah 28:17; Amos 7:7-8) It is far above, and far more stable and true than, the doctrines and theologies of man. Theology is the study of God. It is very important. But see who is doing the studying: man. Which means said study is subject to man – and clearly not to God. We need to be very careful with this.

It is the study *of* God, not the study *by* God. And therein lies the rub. It is intended to be theology – and not theology-ology. It is the study of God, and distinctly not the study of the study of God. A friend of mine says it this way: When you go to the restaurant and you study the menu to determine what you will order, do you eat the menu?! The answer is obvious, and so is the application.

The Word, as important as it is, is not the end. It is the _means_ to the end. The end is the reason for our existence in the first place. The Word is the means of gaining and growing in the richness of relationship, of personal connection to and with the Creator, the Lord our God. It has been referred to as the operator's manual. And that is exactly what it is. It gives us the insights and understandings, the directions and course corrections that put us on track for that deep, deep thing with God.

Herein is seen the vital need of Holy Spirit, who is the Teacher, (Luke 12:12; John 14:26; 1 Corinthians 2:13; 1 John 2:27) and the Counselor, (John 14:16, 14:26, 15:26) and the Guide. (John 16:13) He is also the Spirit of Truth. (John 14:17) With all this in mind, it is essential to make the decision to yield and submit to him. We tend to be impressed by, and settle into, our own intellect, our own wisdom. We hear or read, and then deduce, and think we know. But without his input and direction, we actually know very little.

> **It is critical to understand that just because one is called to leadership does not mean that their will is God's will.**

Forty some years ago it was Chuck Swindoll who said, "The longer I walk with God, the less I know for sure."[2] He was not saying that his knowledge and understanding were dwindling. He was saying that in light of his continued expansion in his relationship with God, which included the truths and understandings of the Word of God, his knowledge was decreasing while God's was increasing in him. So, he was realizing that in and of himself he actually knew very little. Think about that...

The truth is that God is Spirit. (John 4:24) Thus, in order to come to full understanding and revelation of him, of his Word, we must have Holy Spirit helping us. 1 Corinthians 2:10b, 12, 14 says, "The Spirit searches all things, even the deep things of God. We have not received the spirit of the world but the Spirit who is from God, that we may understand what God has freely given us. The man without the Spirit does not accept the things that come from the Spirit of God, for they are foolishness to him, and he cannot understand them, because they are spiritually discerned." We must learn the truths in the Word from Holy Spirit. Period. Then we are in right standing, in right understanding, perspective, and place.

Said another way, there are those who work to discern the Word, and offer up what they think they know, from within their own intellect. And from that do themselves, and the rest of us, a grave disservice. This is also as old as dirt. The worlds of academia and scholarly intellectuality are full of this. But there is a truth that comes from the Truth that he desires us to capture and live within. It is to apprehend and to understand in the manner that comes only by the Spirit, and is understood only by our spirit…

Part of this is to recognize that it is essential that we don't proof-text; it only ends up confusing people and getting us in trouble. Proof-texting is taking the text out of its context so as to support our perspective, our argument, our agenda, our theology.

**It is very important that we don't bring the text to us,
but that we allow the Spirit of God to bring us to the text.**

We yield; the Spirit, the Word does not. Then, and only then, will we come to the fullness of the text, to the truth of the matter.

It is also very important not to yield to traditions. They are just that: traditions. Webster defines tradition as this: "The handing down of stories, beliefs, customs, from generation to generation; a long-established custom or practice that has the effect of an unwritten law; an unwritten religious code."[3] Webster's Encyclopedic

Dictionary adds the words "statements" and "legends" to the mix and says they are handed down from generation to generation, by word of mouth or by practice.[4]

They are created and formulated *by man*, often in spite of what the Word has to say. We must learn not to do that, but rather to yield to the Word. Truth is not relative. It is not adjustable to someone's ideas or interpretations. It is, again, the solid and stable heart of the Creator. Period. Who are we to think we can adjust it to our way of thinking, our way of elucidation?

The Lord will help us if we ask. Weigh and measure the differences, again, with the Lord's help. Build your house on the rock – and distinctly not on the sand. Jesus, the Living Word, is the rock. Man's ways, his thoughts, ideas, perspectives, actions – and traditions - are the sand. Come to this, over and over and over again:

**From God's perspective, answer this: What
does GOD have to say about it,
about whatever is the point of thought,
pursuit, action or challenge?**

I told my wife once that the next time we owned a dog I was going to name it Theology. Then when it did something wrong, I could say, "Bad, Theology!" This because there is so very much of it out there![5] I have done much by way of marriage counseling, business and ministry coaching and consulting over time. Too often, the root of the issues at hand come down to bad theology. It comes down to wrong, incorrect, and sometimes even inappropriate understanding and then application of the Word. It is sad, really, because it does not have to be that way.

It was Rick Joyner, some time ago while teaching on things prophetic, who said this, "There is the receiving of a word [in this case the Word, Scripture]. Then there is the interpretation of what was heard [what was read]. And then there is the application of what was interpreted. The problem is most often not in the hearing [or the reading]. The problem is most often in the interpretation. Which results in a mis-application."[6] (Brackets mine) It is not unlike a computer system, with the reality of "garbage in, garbage out."

The bottom-line question is this: Are you teachable? Can God get into your head and heart and have his way with his Word? Or are you stubbornly stuck in your dogma, your traditions? Can we let God lead? Can we stop thinking the way we thought, acting the way we acted? Can we stop thinking of Church as we have known it? And start thinking of Church as God has defined it? Can we come fully into the reality of Kingdom understanding and living, with his lead, with lordship, et al, and see the bigger picture? Or will we remain stuck?

I think Tozer says it well:

> "Sound Bible exposition is *an imperative must* in the Church of the Living God. Without it no church can be a New Testament church in any strict meaning of that term. But exposition may be carried on in such a way as to leave the hearers devoid of any true spiritual nourishment whatever. For it is not mere words that nourish the soul, but God Himself, and unless and until the hearers find God in personal experience, they are not the better for having heard [what some might classify as] the truth. [It is crucial to understand and embrace that] the Bible is not an end in itself, but a means to bring men to [a brokenness of their own ideas and agendas so they can grow into] an intimate and satisfying knowledge of God; that they may enter into Him, that they may delight in His Presence, may taste and know the inner sweetness of the very God Himself in the core and center of their hearts."[7] (Emphasis and brackets mine.) From this

comes right and correct understanding, and from that comes right theology.

I will end this chapter with these thoughts:

From the New Testament, in Matthew 16:18, we find the word "church" used for the first time. The Greek word is *ekklesia*. There has been much written about this word, its meanings, and its applications. (See Recommended Reading at the end of this book.) My point here is not to replicate but simply to say this:

The word is a compound word, coming from two other Greek words. They are *ek*, which denotes "origin" and means "from." The other is *kaleo*, which is "to call" and this most often out loud. This second word finds its roots in yet another Greek word, which means "to urge on" or "to incite by [audible] word."[8] (Brackets mine) The inference here is one of open communication. It must be seen and understood that this only happens in the midst of community, of relationship. And this with the understanding that we must leave it right there. It is relational; the word church and its application to life is based on, and lives in relationship. It is not based and built on religion, on an established list of rules, regulations, and traditions. Man brought it to that a long time ago, but Father never created it or intended it to be so. This is so essential, so critical to capture.

CHAPTER FIVE

SOLUTION THREE: IDENTIFYING THAT WHICH STANDS IN THE WAY

As we continue forward to address solutions to the problem at hand, to the problems we all face in the context of life with Jesus and life within the ministries we are all called to, we come to the place of recognition. We do well to not only consider the external elements that need to be adjusted, but also those internal issues of the heart that limit, restrict, or otherwise prevent us from all to which we are called, both outwardly and inwardly. We do well to humble ourselves and allow Holy Spirit to reveal all that stands in our way.

One of our biggest challenges is that we think we know. We think we have all the answers. It is now so common to hear, in response to a question or a suggestion, "I know that." And yet there is reason for the question to be asked! The man or woman who lives there is in trouble. The one who has all the answers, who thinks he has all the answers, is no longer teachable. That is a dangerous place to live, my friend. "God resists the proud, but gives grace to the humble." (James 4:6b, NKJV) The expression or position of being non-teachable is one of pride. Instead, let's allow him his work in us.

We raised four wonderfully active children, born close together so they could learn to share life with all its variables. In our county, there were two very large parks that were amazing in scope and variety, each a reflection of the other. It was as if a mechanical engineering team was given free rein to think like children and create as vastly as they could possibly imagine.

Every type and kind of play equipment was brought into the mix, creating a plethora of wonder and delight for any and all who would partake. Large, long slides and tubes to slide down and through to freedom. Bars of all kinds of wonderful shapes and sizes to climb and conquer. Zip lines and swings, large and small, so as to fly into the wind and meet it head-on. A very large, sand-bottomed pond just deep enough to splash, romp, and play in without much risk. Umbrellas, picnic tables, and fire pits to enjoy a meal in the afternoon sun. There was all of this and much, much more to play away the day. It was delightful!

Years later, having moved on to a different location, I awoke to a dream one morning that included this park in all its grandeur. In the dream, the Lord showed me a little boy sitting on one of the diggers, scooping and moving sand from one pile to another and back again. He sat there for quite some time. This was not because he was content, but because he was lacking the spark, the joy, the confidence, and from that the motivation needed to discover and explore the rest of the park. It could have been that he was simply unaware, but that was not it. *He was simply afraid to venture out.* As I watched this young boy, the Lord began to show me that this scene was the exact condition of the Church at large. He said, "My Kingdom is so vast, so amazing, so delightful. I have created so much for all of you. I have so much love for you, all of you who will receive. I have so much desire to share with you, and for all of us together. And yet so many who know me do not partake."

Stuck. So many are so stuck. It's a sad testimony.

In all my years walking with Jesus, with all the awe and wonder, with all the struggles, hardships, and difficulties, I have come fully to the understanding that this walk with him is intended to be an *adventure.* Allow me to unpack that statement:

I came to know Jesus in my late twenties, with my wife by my side. I came from a sordid background with significant pain and woundedness. The transformation from heathen to heaven was overwhelmingly amazing and remarkable. It was not heaven literally, but it certainly was quite heavenly. Jesus saved me from myself and from all the consequences of all my actions and reactions throughout the years. I quickly fell in love. I quickly fell into a love relationship that to this day has never ceased to amaze me, to repeatedly overwhelm me. I have come to know the wonder of who he is, the wonder of his love. As he has so patiently and graciously worked with me and all my inner turmoil, I have also come to clearly see the difficulties of this life, both those I have created and those that have been exercised against me. Within the whole of that came, and still remains, this wonder and an understanding of the *relational adventure* he created and has invited all of us to join him in.[1]

I share this story because it hits home where many people, and many leaders, find themselves today. Stuck. And very far away from any sense of adventure. Burnout. Hope deferred. Loss of vision. Sick, physically or mentally, or both. Marital and family problems. And often from these, elements of unforgiveness and bitterness toward people and God. The list goes on and on. There is no criticism or condemnation here, just observations and concerns.

If one will choose to walk in this way of lordship and total yieldedness and alignment with his Word, his way, then it is time to ask these questions – and find answers. Just what is it that has been standing in the way:

- of this deeper walk?

DR. JAY SLIFE

- of you letting go of you, of self, with all its entrails and trappings, and yielding and submitting to the Lord completely and in fullness?
- of entering into the depth of relationship, the intimacy he is looking and asking for with you?

If one is actually going to engage and live in this place of a new and different way and means of life, and of ministry, one must do their part – which starts with the answers to these questions.

"It is painful business to get through into the stride of God. It means getting your second wind spiritually. And what is it that brings about that second wind? What is it that brings a return of zeal and hunger for the things of God? My friend, it is simple: It is a spirit of obedience!"[2]

It is essential to see the fruit, the result, of this type of life. The value of the fruit is well beyond the ability to measure. It does, however, come at an amazingly high price. The fruit of this lifestyle is found, in part, in Galatians 5:22-23 and is commonly referred to as the Fruits of the Spirit. They are the genuineness, purity, and delight found in love, joy, peace, patience, kindness, goodness, faithfulness, gentleness, and self-control. These are found when we yield and allow him to help us live there.

It is also essential to see the other type of fruit. The fruits of the flesh, found in Galatians 5:19-21, are primarily human traits and conditions that stand in the way of the deeper things of God. It should be noted that they are also points of entry and leverage for the enemy to work. These must be addressed, faced, and dealt with. But not just by self, for that will produce very little fruit – except an increase in performance mentality.

Rather, what is required is this: Repentance. Righteous response to Holy Spirit's convictions. Honesty and integrity before God and man. Confession. Renunciation. Transparency. Openness. Vulnerability. These must be allowed to play out, to become a significant part of one's life.

"When asked what constitutes *success* in life, few believers define success in spiritual terms, [in terms wherein God is the one who defines this for us]. Most describe outcomes related to professional achievement, family solidarity, physical accomplishments, or resource acquisition."[3] (Emphasis and brackets mine.) What a sad testimony.

There are a number of things that can stand in the way of what your Lord wants to do in and through you. Let's look at a few.

The first thing that stands in the way is a mindset that, truthfully, is rooted in stubbornness and independence. These two elements of our humanness actually have their root in pride and rebellion. Independence is essentially nothing more than the right mix of pride and rebellion. Think about it. Stubbornness is the same. Just tweak the ratio and it shifts from one to the other. We want it our way. We want to be in charge. It is where we feel the safest and most secure. We will dig in our heels. We will become spiteful. We will resist the convictions and the promptings of Holy Spirit. Because we are proud and rebellious. But this is not God's way...

The second thing is the undermining and overwhelming reality of fear. Fear of fear itself. Uncertainty. Insecurity. Cowardice. These are all elements of fear. Fear of the unknown. Fear of change. Fear of man, which is fear of the actions and reactions of others. Fear of failure. Fear of success. They all accomplish the same thing. They all steal from us the healthy perspectives, the healthy energies we need to carry forth – in faith, in life, and in ministry. They freeze us in our tracks. But this is not God's way...

Lastly, there are the elements of apathy and lethargy. Both of which, in my country, have a principality attached to, and behind, them. In some ways, they rule the land. And there is the previously mentioned lack of courage, which is cowardice, which also has a principality attached to, and behind, it. These three have developed quite a realm of lack, both individually and corporately. Lack of a sense of value, purpose, and adventure. Lack of joy, which brings a lack of focus and perspective. And a lack of intentionality with Jesus. And, once more, this is not God's way…

All of these things can and do stand in the way. And here, then, is the solution; in my estimation and experience, the only solution: *Enthuo*.

This is a Greek word which is not found in Scripture, but the essence of it is found profusely in the lives of many therein. No more so than in the life of Jesus. The word is *enthuo*. In English, we get the word "enthusiasm" from it. But that is not what it means! It literally means, "to be possessed by a god." It comes from two words, one meaning *in* and the other meaning *god*, so, *in god*. In English, it used to mean, "inspired, intense or eager interest, zeal, fervor."[4] That is very close to the true meaning. When one is possessed, they would manifest elements of those words. But there is more…

Perhaps the best example of this word in action is found in the life of Jesus. In Mark 3:22 it says, "…the teachers of the law who came down from Jerusalem said, 'He is possessed by Beelzebub! By the prince of demons he is driving out demons.'" They are accusing him of being demon-possessed; and this is not the only time they made such an accusation.

A sidebar: This is a very difficult moment in the life of our Savior and Lord. Just one verse earlier, Mark 3:21, his family "… went to take charge of him, for they said, 'He is out of his mind.'" Thus, he is being accused and accosted by his own family and by the teachers of the law at the same time. In public. Put yourself in his sandals for just a moment and see how challenging that would be. In the natural realm, the ultimate of embarrassments and the ultimate of rejections. …ah, but he knew his Father…

The truth of the matter is that Jesus was possessed. But not by demons. He was overwhelmingly caught up in his passion, fervor, and zeal for his Father in heaven. He was possessed. But not by a god. He was possessed by his God, by The God! *Enthuo* was not just a word in his life. It was his lifestyle, his entire way of life. And, again, he is our example.

I offer this word, and the dynamics of its meaning, for one reason: To live a life of *enthuo* is to rise above all of the problematic, arduous, tiring, and complicated things of life previously mentioned in this chapter. Here is the truth: The only way *around* these things is *through* them. They are not solved, resolved, or fully dealt with except by working through them. The manner, and I am suggesting the only manner, in which one can successfully accomplish that, and rise above these issues, is by way of *enthuo*. And since Jesus modeled this for us, he is more than willing to help us in it.

Where is your head? Where is your heart? Where is your thought-life and your attitude? Are you stuck? Stuck in the struggles and doldrums that have come your way by way of choices – or by simply being here, simply living life? Enthuo, my friend. Enthuo. But not by way of performance. By way of crying out and asking, of being broken, of allowing the Spirit of God to have his way. Fully and completely.

The challenging and yet wonderful reality of John 14:30 *must* be weighed and measured, seen for what it is, prayed into, and lived out. "...the ruler of this world [the devil] is coming; he has nothing [no grounds for any accusation] on me..." (NASB, brackets mine.) Our God does not expect perfection from us. He does expect us to "listen and obey and do it right away."[5] He does expect us, based on his investment in and involvement with us, to follow his lead and grow into his image, his likeness. With his help this is possible. It is not a performance thing. It is a relational thing.

I will end this chapter here: In Joshua 1, Yahweh says to Joshua three times, "Be strong and courageous." (Joshua 1:6, 7, 9b) And then to add more emphasis, in one of those statements he adds the word, "very." He goes on to say, "Do not be terrified; do not be discouraged, for the Lord your God will be with you wherever you go." (Joshua 1:9c)

It is very important to see that Yahweh is not calling Joshua out because he is weak and cowardly. Not in the slightest. He is simply – and please catch this – speaking to Joshua about what is already in him. At this point in time, he has spent eighty years with his God. He has been well trained and well prepared for what is about to happen. By way of exhortation, Father God is simply reminding him of that; reminding him of who – and whose – he is.

Is it not the same with you and me? Whether you are a leader or a follower, whether you lead a small group, a church, a denomination, or none of the above there is a new and continuing offer on the table. There is a new, significant, and powerful season upon us.

And there is a God, present and accounted for, who wants you fully engaged in it.

You choose.

CHAPTER SIX

SOLUTION FOUR: UNDERSTANDING YOUR PURPOSE

N ow we turn a corner, one of several we will turn in our journey along this path. Now we come to the first place of application, an application that carries one well outside of self. What is found in this chapter is what I would call critical. Critical in that it casts some vision for all that follows. When we truly understand our purpose, the purpose that comes from the Father, we gain vision and motivation; we gain the *enthuo* that was spoken of in the previous chapter.

I was once invited into a cluster of house church entities to consult, teach, and to speak prophetically, should the Lord direct. Early on in this assignment I was in one of the homes, the leader of which was a man with good intentions. As I walked in the door Father gave me a clear word for this man and the work he was doing within his group: green concrete! I brought the word to him and his wife after the meeting was over and all had left his home.

This was a very difficult word to deliver – and no doubt an even more difficult word to hear. Concrete does not come out of the cement truck green in color. Green concrete is concrete that looks and flows like normal concrete when wet but, for one of several reasons, has not been properly mixed, so it does not properly cure. The net result is concrete that looks normal but has little or no structural integrity. So, after it sets, and when it is subjected to the weight and pressure that comes from what is built upon it, it crumbles and fails. The subsequent result can be disastrous, as all may well come tumbling down, not always immediately but over time. The challenge is to recognize the "greenness" before it is put into service.

You can see the ramifications of this when brought into a leadership role, or really anywhere in one's life. If the foundation upon which one is building and basing their life experience is cemented in green concrete, it will not hold up and stand strong when exposed to weight and pressure. The consequences of that in the realm of any ministry, any investment into the lives of others, can be grievous at best and devastating at worst.

We're not talking about a building that has failed in some manner. We're talking about people and their lives, about something that is not a commodity but has eternal value, certainly in the eyes of God, hopefully in the eyes of those who work for Him. Although this man's intentions were good, his lack of character, inner strength, and ability to healthily withstand life's pressures were bringing he, his wife and family, and his ministry down. A close, prophetic look into his marriage and family revealed large cracks. His weak character was damaging the hearts and lives of those following his lead.

I am not sharing this story to bring shame or condemnation to this man. I am sharing to illustrate what readily happens to any of us who has built, or are building, a life, a ministry, not based on the full and complete truths and principles of the Word, according to the Spirit of the Lord. Built fully as He intends, life will take on the full intention and extension of the Father. Built on some incomplete or partial understanding or theology, or some other base or foundation, it will prove to be green concrete and will crack and crumble, and that which was built upon it will most often come to some very difficult, even disastrous conclusion.[1]

We do well to see the following questions and come to their answers according to the Creator of it all, and not according to our own understandings or experiences. Proverbs 3:5-6 says, "Trust in the Lord with all your heart and lean not on your own understanding; in all your ways acknowledge him, and he will make your paths straight [he will direct your paths.]" (Brackets mine)

1.   What is our purpose, our objective, and thus our goal?

Is it not to follow him in all manner of life, to live life as he has created and intended it to be lived? Is it not to honor him and serve him all the days of our lives according to his ways? Is it not to bless him and worship him by way of yieldedness and submission so as to acknowledge and allow his persona, his glory, to rule and reign on earth as it is in heaven? "He must increase, but I must decrease." (John the Baptist speaking, John 3:30)

Is it not the Great Commandment? (Matthew 22:37-40) Which paraphrased is, "To love the Lord our God with all our heart, soul, mind, and strength. And to love others so they can do the same." Isn't that what it all boils down to? Isn't that exactly why we were created in the first place? So then, isn't it about the Great Commandment coupled with the Great Commission (Matthew 28:18-20); the second being worthless without the first? But the two together having more power and significance than any other directive on the planet?

Again, isn't that where we find our purpose, our value? In all honesty, isn't it that which we find burning in our hearts? The social gospel, the watered down and twisted "woke" gospel, the compromised warm-fuzzy gospel; these are well represented in today's world. But they totally miss the mark and muddy the waters. The true gospel speaks to Jesus the Christ and to his Kingdom. It speaks to real life, to life now and for eternity. It speaks to the tangible reality of the true love of God for his creation, all eight billion of us. In that truth is found our purpose and so our goal.

2. In the context of purpose, what one fights for or against is a clear indicator of what is important to them. So, what are we fighting for and against?

Are we not fighting for the King to rule and reign within his Kingdom? Are we not fighting for all of the broken people and broken relationships within families, communities, and even countries? Including our own? Are we not fighting for all the broken value systems/paradigms/worldviews to be changed and aligned with the heart of our God? And of his Kingdom? I think so.

Are we not fighting for the delightful brokenness of humility and patience that comes from a deep, sweet relationship with our Lord and Savior? And also fighting against the brokenness of man, by man? Within which is found the work of the enemy? Again, I think so.

In the beginning, God created the heavens and the earth, all for the purpose of relationship. Then they, Father, Son, and Holy Spirit, created mankind in their image, their likeness, all for the purposes of relationship, then, now, and forever. They gave the earth to their creation, to humans. After we fumbled it away, and our souls with it, Jesus came and took it all back - and gave it to us again, with him in the mix this time. All for the purpose of relationship.

On the other side of this bubble we call time, at the end of this story, there is a wedding, complete with a wedding feast around a banqueting table; wait for it... all for the purpose of relationship. There the bridegroom will delightfully embrace, capture, and marry his bride, and off into eternity they will go. It is the most amazing love scene in all of time and history; truthfully, in all of eternity. The angels can hardly wait! It will be the only scene in the history of scenes, in all of time, that truly ends with them living happily ever after. All other similar scenes are just a novel, a movie, or a theatrical performance; not reality.

"Why is this all true and real? One more time: all for the purpose of relationship. We have been created to worship God in spirit and in truth, which is from the core of our souls, and to share his love and good news with others so they can do the same. Period. All of the other things we do, or are a part of, have value, but none of them are the reason. They are simply a means to an end, the end being his purposes and intentions."[2]

Please capture this:

All that the Creator of the Universe, the Almighty God of Heaven and Earth, the Pursuer and the Lover of your soul, has ever wanted, has ever accomplished, from beginning to end, *he has done from the place of love, from the place of desire for relationship with those he loves.* His heart's desire is simply that and nothing more. He is passionately and overwhelmingly in love with his creation, with you and me. Why did God create the earth? For you. Why did he establish people, you and me, on his earth? Because of his capacity for, and desire to, love. Because he wanted a bride for his

Son. Because he wanted a love relationship, true, deep, and rich for his Son; and from there for himself.

"The truth is you take his breath away, you overwhelm him; he cannot stop himself. He created and built it all for you. He is all in for you. Forever. But not just for you. For all of the yous on the planet. Had there have been just one you, he would have done it the same. But he wants all the yous."[3]

Is this not what we fight for, live for, breathe for? If not, then why not? From Job: "I am God and you are not." Since that is the truth, and since he created us as he has, and since he sent his Son Jesus to make it all right between us, we owe it to him to honor and respect him, to love him back. Which means we live in the dynamics of relationship, lordship, and stewardship according to him and his way of defining all of that.

Let's get to this. Let's be part of the people who are becoming insistent on getting back to this. Let's come into alignment with God's purposes for us and "press on toward the mark of the prize of the high calling in Christ Jesus." (Philippians 3:14)

**"Everything flows out of intimacy with
God and with one another."[4]**

PART TWO

THE NEW TESTAMENT MODEL: THE ARGUMENT FOR HOUSE CHURCHES

CHAPTER SEVEN

THE ASSUMPTION OF
THE KINGDOM OF GOD

She came into our Gathering very low in countenance. It was obvious she had been crying. She was a regular part of our group, a fire-ball of sorts with a strong love for Jesus. I took a deep breath, and listened for the Lord to speak. Upon asking her what was going on she shared that the diagnosis was final. She had a disease in her eyes that was unstoppable and irreversible. She was losing her eye sight and would eventually go blind, this in her latter twenties. I immediately heard the Lord say, "Pray." So, we gathered around her, laid hands on her, and prayed, asking for a total and complete healing. She was healed in that moment!

Fast forward ten years. I bumped into her at a restaurant where we were both there with friends. I had not seen her in quite a while. In the context of some brief interchange, I asked her about her eyes. Her healing was complete at the moment we prayed over her, and had remained to that day. Supernatural Healing.

In a different encounter, I was with a friend from our Home Gathering, standing in line waiting our turn to order coffee. As I turned to the cashier to order, the Lord gave me a Word of Knowledge for her. I paused a moment to be sure he wanted me to bring it to her in that moment. He confirmed. I put the Word in the form of a question. She was a bit taken back by the question but did answer. As she was answering, the Lord gave me a second Word of Knowledge. I put this one in the form of a question as well. He gave me a total of four Words for her, all delivered with a question, each one probing deeper into her soul. She answered all four and by the fourth one she was quite shaken, slightly fearful, and crying. And all of her co-workers had stopped what they were doing and were watching. And wondering.

After a few moments, as you might imagine, things started to get awkward. We ordered our drinks and moved on. When I went to pick up the drinks, she was standing there with the drinks in her hands, her co-workers watching. (Sidebar: If you know anything about the high-volume coffee shop business, you know that each worker stays within their assignment. The cashier taking orders does not fill the order; nor does she connect with the customer to deliver. That is for the next person in their system to do.) I don't know if she made them, but she was there to deliver them – and had them in her control. She was not letting those drinks go until she talked with me.

With tears in her eyes, she said, "You have no idea. You have no idea what you just did to me. I have been crying out for years for instruction and direction for my life. I have been trying to find God and his will for my life, and in two minutes you have turned my entire life upside down." I helped her to understand that what was happening was not me, that Holy Spirit had given me those four Words of Knowledge, and I had put them in the form of questions. Then, in that moment, he continued on in his ministry to her by giving me a prophecy for her, which I delivered.

She was totally undone by the love and compassion – and power - of God. And she had her answers to the prayers that she had been praying all those years. Oh, and she then gave me my drinks! Words of Knowledge. Prophecy. Wow.

I could go on. God is spirit, a supernatural being. (John 4:24) And he delights in manifesting himself in the lives of his creation in that manner. Much of this has been lost over time, but the God of the Universe still loves to minister to his people, and often supernaturally. As has already been stated in Chapter One, he also delights in using his people to minister to his people. This is his heart at work. This is his Kingdom at work. And this is his preferred methodology for living life with his people. If we learn to be Spirit-filled and from that Spirit-led, we can and will live here. The story of the little boy digging in the sand at the county park in Chapter Five comes to mind. He was stuck -- but we don't have to be. This can be quite exciting and adventurous! Let's let him take us there!

In all likelihood, the Gospel of Mark is the first book of the Gospels written. Thus, what follows would be the first words Jesus spoke publicly. "The Gospel according to Mark begins the story of Jesus' ministry with these significant words: 'Jesus came into Galilee, preaching the gospel [the good news] of God, saying,

> ***'The time is fulfilled, and the Kingdom of God is at hand;***

repent and believe in the gospel' (1:14-15). [With this proclamation,] Mark thus makes it plain that the burden of Jesus' preaching was to announce the Kingdom of God; that it was *the central thing with which he was concerned.* Everywhere [he traveled] the Kingdom of God [was] on his lips, and it [was] always a matter of desperate importance. What is it like? How does one enter? Is it [really] a matter of importance?"[1] (Emphasis and brackets mine) And, yes, it most certainly is!

We need to be operating under a particular assumption, which will bring us to a particular conclusion. We need to capture the broad and deep understanding that the King and his Kingdom are the core of all that we are and ever can be. All else comes from this. We need to understand that this, and this alone, is what we have been created and called to. Please re-read this paragraph, and let it sink in.

[A side-bar just for you: Get back to the Gospels. They are placed first in the New Testament for a reason. They are of the utmost importance; especially in the days in which we live.]

The word *Kingdom* is used one-hundred-fourteen times in the Gospels, fifty-two times just in the book of Matthew. (NIV) In that same context, the word church is used twice. That alone speaks volumes to its importance. Jesus came to Earth for several reasons.

Yes, one of them was to establish the Church, but that came later in his ministry. It was the Kingdom that came first. It is essential to understand that one of his primary purposes for coming to earth was to usher in the Kingdom of God. He came to model and express the Kingdom of God for us. His intention was to invite us in, not to observe but to serve, not to simply perceive it but to walk in it and live it out. The Church is not the Kingdom; it is not equal to the Kingdom. It is but a part of the Kingdom. The model of life, of ministry, of the advancement of the Gospel, is not the Church. It is the Kingdom of God. Period.

Stop thinking Church. Start thinking Kingdom.

**This is imperative for where the Lord wants to take us.
It is also imperative for the type of ministry
to which he has called us.**

Regarding this Kingdom, George Eldon Ladd captured the dilemma we are in well when he said, "When we ask the Christian Church, 'What is the Kingdom of God? When and how will it come?' we receive a bewildering diversity of explanations."[2] I think this statement is quite accurate, and also, quite understated.

The Kingdom of God is complex to define; it is much more caught than taught. If I ask you to define with words the color red or the dynamics of love, you would find it quite difficult. However, when you experience red or love it is much easier to express. There have been hundreds of volumes written about the King and his Kingdom. None of them bring full definition or understanding to it. It has to be experienced to be understood. At some point, talk actually diminishes the value of whatever is being discussed. The man waxes eloquent trying to describe his love for his bride – while she leans in close and whispers, "Just kiss me." And the long, intimate kiss says more than all the expressive and fluent words added together. There is no way to express that kiss in words. Ah, but the experience of it rocks their world. So it is with the Kingdom. There is the intense need for understanding, with the heart and not simply with the mind. We are called to live out this truth; we must choose to do so.

Basically, an initial definition is that the Kingdom of God is the *rule* and the *reign*, of God; and from that, the *realm* of God. The King has a Kingdom and the Kingdom has a King. Go figure. "The Kingdom of God is the rule of God and is both a present reality and a future hope. The idea of God's Kingdom is *central* to Jesus' teaching."[3] (Emphasis mine)

"The Kingdom is a present reality, and yet a future blessing. (Matthew 12:28; 1 Corinthians 15:50) It is an inner spiritual redemptive blessing which can be experienced only by way of the new birth, and yet [it is so vast that] it will have to do with the government[s] of the nations of the world. (Romans 14:17; John 3:3; [Isaiah 9:6-7]; Revelation 11:15) The Kingdom is a realm into which men enter now, and yet it is a realm into which they will enter tomorrow [in eternity]. (Matthew 21:31, 8:11) It is at the same time a gift of God which will be bestowed by God in the future and yet which must be received [and lived out] in the present. (Luke 12:32; Mark 10:15) Obviously, no simple explanation can do justice to such a rich but diverse [reality]."[4] (Brackets mine)

Further understanding of the Kingdom of God can be gained by simply defining the word *kingdom* from the original languages. Today we think that a kingdom is "a realm over which a king exercises his authority." Or we think of a kingdom as "the people belonging to [such a] realm." However, these definitions can lead us down an errant path. "The English dictionary itself makes this mistake when it gives as the theological definition of *kingdom*, 'the spiritual realm having God as its head.' This definition cannot do justice to the verses which speak of the Kingdom [now or in the future]. Furthermore, those who begin with the idea of the Kingdom as a people base their definition upon the identity of the Kingdom with the Church, and for this there is very little scriptural warrant."[5] (Brackets mine) This is another substantial understatement.

"The primary meaning of both the Hebrew... and the Greek words for *kingdom* ...is the rank, authority, and sovereignty exercised by a king. [These words] may indeed be a realm over which a sovereign [being] exercises his authority; and it may be the people who belong to that realm and over whom authority is exercised; but these are secondary and derived meanings. First of all, [first and foremost,] a kingdom is the authority to rule, the sovereignty of the king. When the word refers to God's Kingdom, it always refers to his reign, his rule, his sovereignty."[6] (Emphasis and brackets mine)

Here are two examples from Ladd from his book, *The Gospel of the Kingdom,* that distinctly contribute to the understanding of our word *kingdom,* one from Scripture and one from Jewish history in the time just before Jesus:

> One reference [to kingdom] in our Gospels makes this meaning very clear. Luke 19:11-12 says, "As they heard these things, he proceeded to tell a parable... He said, 'A nobleman went into a far country to receive a kingdom and then return.' The nobleman did not go away to get a realm, an area over which to rule. The realm over which he wanted to reign was at hand. The territory over which he was to rule was this place he left. The problem was that he was no king. He needed authority, the right to rule. He went off to get a kingdom, i.e., kingship, authority. [And when he returned, he had been made king, verse 15.]

> This very thing actually happened years before the days of our Lord. In the year 40 BC political conditions in Palestine had become chaotic. The Romans had subdued the country, ...but stability had been slow in coming. Herod the Great finally

went to Rome, obtained from the Roman Senate the kingdom, and was declared to be king. He literally went into a far country to receive a kingship, the authority to be king in Judea over the Jews. This illustrates the fundamental meaning of kingdom.

The Kingdom of God is his kingship, his rule, his authority. When this is once realized, we can go through the New Testament and find passage after passage where this meaning is evident, where the Kingdom is not a realm or a people, but God's reign. Jesus said that we must 'receive the kingdom of God' as little children (Mark 10:15). What is received? The Church? Heaven? What is received is God's rule.[7]

Think about it; this truth is clearly seen in something we are very familiar with: the Lord's prayer. "When we pray, …what we are praying for is '*Thy kingdom come, thy will be done* on earth as it is in heaven.' This prayer is a petition for God to reign, to manifest his kingly sovereignty and power, to put to flight every enemy of righteousness and of his divine rule, [human or demonic] that God alone may be King over all the world."[8] (Emphasis and brackets mine)

Once his rule and reign is understood, we must realize that in the overall context of the sovereign God there is also a realm within which he can implement his rule. "…a reign without a realm in which it is exercised is meaningless. Thus, we find that the Kingdom of God is also the realm in which God's reign may be experienced."[9] The rule, the reign, and the realm…

In all my research, this is the strongest and most concise argument regarding the Kingdom I have ever come across. It also comes from Ladd's book, *The Gospel of the Kingdom:*

- "'Repent, for the kingdom of heaven is at hand.' (Matthew 4:17)
- This theme of the coming of the Kingdom of God was *central* in his mission. His teaching was designed to show men how they might enter the Kingdom of God. (Matthew 5:20, 7:21)
- His mighty works were intended to prove that the Kingdom of God had come upon them. (Matthew 12:28)
- His parables illustrated to his disciples the truth about the Kingdom of God. (Matthew 13:11)
- And when he taught his followers to pray, at the heart of their petition were the words, 'Thy kingdom come, thy will be done on earth as it is in heaven.' (Matthew 6:10)
- On the eve of his death, he assured his disciples that he would yet share with them the happiness and the fellowship of the Kingdom. (Luke 22:22-30)
- And he promised that he would appear again on the earth in glory to bring the blessedness of the Kingdom to those for whom it was prepared. (Matthew 25:31,34)
- ...the Kingdom of God is a present spiritual reality. 'For the kingdom of God is not eating and drinking but righteousness and peace and joy in the Holy Spirit. (Romans 14:17) Righteousness and peace and joy are fruits of the Spirit of God which God bestows now upon those who yield their lives to the rule of the Spirit. They have to do with the deepest springs of the spiritual life, *and this is the Kingdom of God.*
- [And then this:] "How can the Kingdom of God be a present spiritual reality and yet be an inheritance bestowed upon God's people at the Second Coming of Christ? ...Kingdom truth reflects the fact that the Kingdom is a *realm* into which the followers of Jesus Christ have entered. Paul, [speaking to believers,] writes that God has 'delivered us from the dominion of darkness and transferred us to the *kingdom*

of his beloved Son.' (Colossians 1:13) This verse makes it very clear that the redeemed are already in the Kingdom of Christ. (The Kingdom of God is also the Kingdom of Christ (Ephesians 5:5; Revelation 11:15; see also Luke 16:16))."[10] (Emphasis and brackets mine)

We do well to understand that, "The Kingdom of God, in Christ, has created the Church, and the Kingdom of God works in the world through the Church to accomplish the divine purposes of extending his Kingdom in the world. We are caught up in a great struggle – the conflict of the ages – this evil age and this gospel of the Kingdom."[11]

I would offer that there is a second great struggle. The primary tool that God has put in place to bring forth the gospel of his Kingdom is the Church. And the Church has seemingly been at odds with itself ever since. This is the strategy of the enemy and he seems to be doing a good job of it. We know he does not win, but we must come to the place where we yield and allow God to re-establish the Church to its rightful place so it can be victorious in its assignment *within his Kingdom.*

I believe the main way in which that will happen is for the Church to get its focus off itself. We spend so much energy focusing on all the things we think are wrong with the other guy. "Cancel culture" is not a new thing within the Church at large; it has been around for centuries. In this the devil wins. Can we mature to the place wherein our focus is on the Author and Finisher of our faith; where our focus is on him and his work? (Hebrews 12:2 KJV) Can we come to the place where we simply submit? And from that follow his lead, and distinctly not our own? And, from that, carry on with our fellow believers in a Christ-like manner?

To reiterate, we must understand that the Kingdom is not a theory or a theology, it is a call to decision, and from there to action. Consider this: "We must also 'seek first his Kingdom and his righteousness.' (Matthew 6:33) What is the object of our quest?

The Church? Heaven? No, we are to seek God's righteousness – his sway, his rule, his reign in our lives."[12]

Matthew 6:33 says, "But seek first the Kingdom of God and his righteousness, and all these things shall be added to you." (NKJV) The NASB says it this way: "But seek first *his* Kingdom and *his* righteousness, and all these things will be added to you." And the Amplified Bible offers this rendition: "But seek (aim at and strive after) first of all his Kingdom and his righteousness (his way of doing and being right), and then all these things taken together will be given you besides." (Emphasis mine) Wuest adds the word *be* for emphasis: "But be seeking first…" His reasoning is based on the voice and the tense of the word in the original Greek manuscripts.[13]

The heartbeat of the Kingdom has been very well encapsulated by Hagner in his book, *Word Biblical Commentary, Volume 33A*:

> This verse concisely states the [emphatic and] climactic point of the entire pericope. [Matthew 6:25-34. A pericope is a section of a book.] The kingdom, and kingdom alone, is to be the *sole priority* of the disciple and that toward which the disciple devotes his or her energy. Seek here does not necessarily mean to look for something not yet present and, given the context of the Gospel, certainly cannot mean one should seek to bring in the kingdom. This imperative [word] means rather that *one should make the kingdom the center of one's existence and thus experience the rule of God fully in one's heart*, hence the present tense, 'keep seeking.'

> To pursue the kingdom in this way is also to seek his righteousness, i.e., true righteousness or that which is truly the will of God as it is defined by the teaching of Jesus. Participation in the kingdom, as Matthew has already informed us, necessitates

righteousness of a qualitatively new kind. The gift of the kingdom and the demand of this new righteousness are inseparable. Thus gift, and not merely demand, is implied in this text. The emphatic "first" or "above all" means to make the kingdom and righteousness one's clear *priority* in life.[14] (Emphasis and brackets mine)

Having now come to a working understanding of the Kingdom of God, there is another facet we need to consider. What does the King and his Kingdom demand from us? What does our place and involvement in his Kingdom ask and require of us? What does that look like? How is it that we get there?

Bright, from his book, *The Kingdom of God*, stated it this way:

...it is clear that Christ summoned men to the Kingdom of the *Servant*. It is a Kingdom of the meek and lowly [Matthew 5:5, 11:29] in which the leader is he who is willing to be 'last of all and servant of all' (Mark 9:35) or, as John records it, (John 13:14-17) who has so little pride that he will consent to wash his fellow's feet. And who is called to that Kingdom? Why, all weary and heavy-laden souls who are willing to take on themselves the gentle yoke of the Servant. (Matthew 11:28-30) It welcomes all humble, kindly men who 'hunger and thirst' for it and who are willing to serve it to the utmost. (Matthew 5:3-12; Luke 6:20-23) Wealth will get no one into it; indeed, wealth has kept many a man out. (Mark 10:17-25) External rectitude [moral or religious correctness] is no ticket of admission; for that the scribes and Pharisees had in plenty, and it is certain that crooks and prostitutes will enter the Kingdom ahead of them. (Matthew

21:31) The Kingdom belongs, in the final analysis, to those who have stripped themselves of all pride – whether of station or of wisdom or of rectitude – and have become as little children – eager to receive. (Mark 10:14)

Nor is the call of [the] Kingdom a call to honor or to victory, as the world understands those terms, but to utter self-denial. Over and over again we hear of the tremendous cost of it. One leaves father and mother, home and family, at its summons, and when one has done so, he may be assured that he will be, like his Lord, a wanderer without where to lay his head. (Matthew 19:29; Mark 10:29; Luke 18:29; Matthew 8:20; Luke 9:58) One will be hated, nay, persecuted. (Matthew 10:22; Mark 13:13; Matthew 5:10-11; Luke 6:22) But there will be no retaliation – only a turning of the other cheek. (Matthew 5:39; Isaiah 50:6) He who heeds the call of the Kingdom has no destiny save to take up his cross and follow the Servant. (Matthew 10:38; Mark 8:34; Luke 14:27) But to those who are called, there is given nothing less than the Servant mission: to proclaim the gospel of the Kingdom to all the nations of the earth."[15] (Emphasis and brackets mine)

This Kingdom, and its call and demand, are where and how we are to live. This Kingdom answers the question of why we are to live. It truly is the core of our reason and purpose in living. Where we are headed in this day and age, with all of the challenges and complexities all around us, requires and demands our adherence to the Christ and his Kingdom. It is that essential. It is that commanding.

As we move into a further understanding of small group ministry – and the call of God therein – it must be understood that to live within this principle necessitates living within the larger principle of the Kingdom of God.

CHAPTER EIGHT

THE ARGUMENT FOR HOUSE CHURCHES

In my first year of bible college, I was given the assignment to determine, "When exactly did the Church come into existence?" It was a very good project for a beginning student, forcing me to research, think, and extrapolate from Scripture just what the answer might be. Was it on the Cross? Or at the Resurrection or the Ascension? Perhaps it was in the Upper Room? Or maybe in the Temple Courtyard? Today, if I was that college professor, I would ask that same question and add two more:

> 1) In terms of practical routine and action; in terms of relationships, vertical and horizontal; in terms of Holy Spirit engagement and involvement; in terms of out-reach and expansion; just exactly what did the first Church look like?

> 2) When did things change from that beginning?

I believe the answer to these two additional questions would bring great revelation and insight.

From the Course Objective for a class I took, "The Church in Europe is closing down; the Church in the U.S. is declining; the Church in China is ceasing to grow; in the Church in South America growth is slowing down; and the African Church is not seeing as much revival. Can we reverse that? Has the passion and vision for the great commission changed or waned and are we seeing progress in our generation? Are we not working strategically or hard enough? Is there somewhere or something that has gone wrong?"[1]

I believe these are great questions and open the door wide open regarding Church issues at large. I believe some of the main reasons the Church is struggling has to do with this: In the natural realm, there is more and more humanism and relativism. There is less and less truth and true relationship based on the absolutes of the God of the Universe. There is more and more of a thrust from both Islam and Communism. And there is less and less effective evangelism and discipleship. In the spiritual realm, there is less of God in the core of life's pursuits and more of the ways of man, of humanity. There is less lordship and more of the creature comforts of mankind. Often God gets either totally removed or seriously reduced to programs, systems, and traditions, while the truth is that we need more of him heart-to-heart.

I think it is way past time to rethink the model of ministry that has been in play for well over seventeen-hundred years, quit trying to polish and re-polish the apple, and work at something different. And recognize that the something different is not so different at all – since it is the original model of ministry, of Church.

This chapter has all to do with revealing the obvious. A clear, unbiased, and thorough study of the New Testament, from Acts through the Epistles, distinctly illuminates the type of ministry that was common in those days. This was first church activity. This is how it started. They met, "in the Temple and from house to house." (Acts 5:42) The Temple was an important part, no doubt. But the main component of life was from house to house. The basic formulation of the Church as we know it today, did not show up in history until the latter two-hundreds. Before that, across Israel and Asia Minor, it was in homes. "The Church was at home where people were at home."[2]

I am not alone when I say that significant research has shown that the early church was truly an expression of the *Kingdom of God*, and its fullest expression was in people's homes and in the streets where they lived. And not just in Israel. Paul and others went about Asia Minor and southern Europe and by way of signs and wonders and personal testimony spread the Gospel and advanced the Kingdom. And, as is not uncommon in the ways of the King, he is bringing us back to where we started. It is coming full circle. An expression of his heart – and a clear indicator of the times in which we live.

With her husband by her side, a woman came forward for prayer. She was having intense headaches that would not go away. Her doctor had prescribed some medication, but it was not working. I was listening to her story while also listening for Holy Spirit to instruct and direct. He said, "Dispel fear." That was it, nothing more, nothing less. When she was done, I said to her, "I hear the Lord saying to dispel fear." With that, I extended my hand toward her forehead and spoke those two words. My hand was more than a foot from her head. Upon me speaking, she flew backward and landed on the floor. Fortunately, her husband was both attentive and quick as he guided her fall to a peaceful landing. He placed his jacket over her, and she laid there for over half an hour. The headaches left and never returned. Her issue was not from a malady in her head. She had become overwhelmed with fear from several circumstances in her life. Holy Spirit knew exactly what she needed – and gladly brought that to her. I never prayed for the headaches! Word of Knowledge. Obedient prayer. Another wow. _This_ is the kind of ministry the Father wants for all of us. It works best in small group environments.

Point blank: This is where Father God wants life lived on planet earth. This is his heart and his intention for his people, his creation. It is where we can live deeply with him and one another. The fullness of relationship and all that he is and offers is no better discovered and engaged than in this setting. It is where the fullness of signs and wonders and spiritual gifts - the Spirit of God manifesting - finds its broadest usage. It is the New Testament model of ministry. Period.

We do well to figure this out. We do well to allow him to change us, to bring us to the beauty and wonder found herein. I have shared a number of stories of his input that have changed and transformed lives. Those are not me or about me. It is simply a man who was offered, and chose to respond to an adventure, to a completely different way of living life. How about you? Are you ready for this?

Obviously, this is my perspective, my opinion on things. It is my experience, and I would not change it for anything. I have seen too much. I have been too involved for too long a period of time to see and understand it differently. So many people and families transformed. Too many people who did not find healing and resolve to their life's issues until they encountered Holy Spirit in the context of small group ministry. Too many encounters with the Living God that just do not happen in any other arena.

If you are reading this book, and have gone this far into its contents, then there is something within you that at least has you curious. I would suggest that that something is someone and his name is Holy Spirit. He is working within your soul to draw you in and help you out. Please continue to allow him to do his work.

With fellow students, in the midst of discussing and debating the "Classical Church Model" and the "House Church Model" from history and Scripture, in the midst of reading a fellow student's assignment, came the following. I felt the Lord gave me a prophetic, directive word for him:

To set the table, in the world of car racing, in the world of horsepower, torque, traction, and fuel efficiency, and the engineering behind all of those factors, one of the primary points of consideration is what is called *horsepower to weight ratio*. (If you have watched the movie *Ford versus Ferrari* then you have seen them struggle through this phenomenon.) Basically, and without getting too technical, the bottom line is that the more horsepower and the less weight the better, because it results in more efficiency and thus more speed. I heard the Lord saying:

"Reduce your weight. You have more than enough horsepower. Reduce your weight and find the fruit,

success, and victory you are looking for. This is not your weight as in your personal weight. This is weight as in the load you have built and are carrying in ministry, in the endeavors you are involved in, and just how you are going about them. This is speaking to the church you lead and the weight it carries, excess weight. You do well to shift to the House Church Model. It offers much less weight, much more traction and thus, more actual fruit from your labors, from your horsepower. The horsepower has all to do with the anointing and resultant authority you carry. Lose the weight and watch the torque and traction, the fuel efficiency and engine performance of your ministry flourish, thrive, and advance."

This is a very timely word. Not just for the gentleman for whom it was initially aimed, but for everyone being pulled by Father to make the shift to this current House Church/Home-Gathering Network endeavor. Please recognize what your Lord is impressing on your heart and has you working on or toward.

The Greek word for *house* in Strong's Concordance takes up over six pages – with a font size that my eyes say is a negative number! If you add *houses* and *household* to the mix, it's another page. In Luke and Acts alone *house* is used ninety-two times. The phrase, "…in the house of…" referring to a church in a house is found nine times in Acts. The phrases, "…the church in the house," or "…that meets in the house…" are found throughout Acts and the Epistles.[3] It was the normal manner of life. When churches were planted, all around the Mediterranean Sea, which was the entire beginnings of the physical and written expression of the Kingdom, they were planted in houses. House churches and the understanding of *house to house* was as common as dirt! (Acts 2:46, NKJV) That is the pattern our Lord had in mind – and has in mind for today and into the future.

Why a house church? Why the whole of house churches around the country, around the globe? Because it reflects the heart of God. And it accomplishes this reflection more than any other option. How far can you go in relationship with the people around you in the meet-and-greet time on a Sunday morning? How good a friend are you to them or them to you? Do they know how much you hurt inside? Or how lonely you are? Or you them?

It is not truly meet-and-greet. It is hide-and-ride. As in I am going to hide behind my façade and ride out the next ninety seconds so I can sit back down and withdraw back into my little world, and hope that my pulse and blood pressure settle back down. Or, it is slip-and-dip, as in I will slip out of bed, stay home, and perhaps dip into whatever the guy on TV has to say today. Sad, but all too true.

The character, the heart of Father God is not there. But it is here: "The house church reflects God's qualities and his character. This community lifestyle is molded in the spirit of love, truth, forgiveness, faith, and grace. In house churches, we love each other, forgive each other, mourn with those who mourn, laugh with those who laugh, extend and receive grace, and constantly remain in touch with God's truth and forgiveness. The house church is a place where all masks can be removed, and where we can be open to one another while still loving each other."[4]

It is that place where we can meet with God at a depth not found anywhere else. It is where we grow and advance in character and life. It is where we can be authentic with ourselves and one another in the presence, in the safety and security, of our Creator. Life's issues are prayed about, prayed into, prayed over, released to him – and solutions found and received through him. This is where he lives in the context of love, compassion, truth, and their many applications to life.

When established and built properly, a house church develops an arena of encouragement, accountability, support, and trust. It is within this parameter that the primary portion of spiritual growth and maturity take place. It is here that we learn to *understand* the scriptures and, even more important, *apply* them to life. It is here that we laugh and cry and face the actualities of life together in Christ, and expose and dispose of the struggles with virtual reality, fantasy, and escapism. It is in this context that we come to terms with truths such as unity and community, power and love, signs and wonders, spiritual gifts and the exercising of same, outreach and up-reach. It is in this place that we learn the true dynamics of interdependency, and total dependency upon our Lord and Savior. It is here that we develop a lifestyle that actually lives the life of a born-again child of the Living God. It is here that we come past the apathy and lethargy, the cowardice and shallowness, of many within the American Church, and grow deep with our Jesus. And it is here that we come to terms with the lordship of Christ in our lives.

Simson captures well this style of ministry. All of these statements reference house churches from his book, *The House Church Book*:

- "Baptized with the Greek pagan philosophy of separating the sacred from the secular, the [Church] system became [and still is] the black hole of Christianity… but until today nobody has really changed the system.
- The church is the people of God. The church, therefore, was and is at home where people are at home: [in their homes].
- The New Testament church was made up of small groups, typically between ten and fifteen people.
- A pastor [shepherd] is an important member of the whole team, but he or she cannot fulfill more than part of the task of equipping the saints.
- We have all the right pieces, but we have fit them together in the wrong way.
- In order to bring about change we need to "enable the priesthood of all believers;" [1 Peter 2:9] the present system will have to change completely.
- Too much organization has the potential of restricting and choking the organism simply out of fear that something might go wrong. Fear wants to control; faith can trust.

- Christians are called to worship in spirit and truth. [John 4:23,24] The Lord's Supper was actually more a substantial meal. God is restoring eating [and fellowshipping over a meal] back into our meetings.
- Authenticity in the neighborhoods connected with a... citywide corporate identity will make the Church... spiritually convincing.
- Unfortunately, contemporary Christianity is often too harmless and polite to be worth persecuting. We need to again begin to live out New Testament standards of life.
- The church [needs to] turn back to its roots – back to where it came from, [the home]."[5](Brackets mine)

The stories I have been sharing throughout this book, the healings and transformations, mostly happened in a house church environment. We live in a fearful climate; there may be more fear on a corporate level today than in most times in our history. That statement is not limited to the US; fear seems to be on the rise all over the world. The direct opposite of fear is love. (1 John 4:18) The direct component to combat fear is trust. Trust itself is hard to build and quick to crumble. There is not even a chance to build it -- except within a small group of people who intentionally work at building it. It simply will not work any other way -- but it is a beautiful thing when it happens.

Allow me to unpack some of the myths and mysteries surrounding house churches. For approximately the first three-hundred years, the church looked a lot like the model found in New Testament scripture. We know that the Greek word, *ekklesia*, translates into English as "church." It was used in three different ways. It was used "in reference to believers gathering in someone's home, the citywide or regional church, and the church universal. It was *never* used in reference to a special building, a religious ceremony, or a class of paid professional leaders. [That all came later.] The [emphasis of the] word [*ekklesia* simply] brings out the importance of clustering, assembling, or meeting together,"[6] It wasn't until Constantine legalized the Christian church in 313 A.D. that all things changed.

Even later, in what we know as the Protestant Reformation, although much was improved, there was still the mistaken principles of pastoral and priestly excessive control. Things changed, but more accurately they merely shifted. Traditions, man-made systems, and the whole of lay -- clergy dynamics still overrode Scripture. The common man still remained common – and uninformed and uneducated to the beautiful wonders of the Triune God. It missed the mark then, and still does.

The early church "lived… out, practically from day to day, …the specific and important functions and forms that worked. The early church minimized the complexity of its forms in order to maximize the effectiveness of its functions." It was simply not caught up in all the formality and grandeur; it was totally caught up in the Christ and his examples of how to live life. "Their beliefs determined their behavior, their function determined their form, their mandate determined their methods."[7]

I think the most important thing to learn from the first church is the fact that it was not just a meeting in a home. It was a *spiritual* meeting in a home. "The apostle Peter characterized believers as living stones fitted together to form a spiritual house *for God's good pleasure*. This spiritual place was a place where a holy priesthood… offer up spiritual sacrifices to God."[8] (Emphasis mine) The focus on the believers, as opposed to some leader, and their intimate connection to God ushered in "a new era characterized by true spiritual worship of God unrestricted by 'holy' locations [or formats.]"[9] (Brackets mine) They were simply real, and what they built to facilitate that was the same: simple and real. As it is intended to be today.

It is also important to understand that *house to house* was not developed because of persecution or poverty or on a temporary basis, as some have taught. "Any reputable history textbook"[10] will reveal that persecution, although real and horrible, was not an overarching reality. And poverty may have been an issue for some, as it is today, but it was not a driving force. And if the leadership was thinking of houses as a temporary idea, then why were they the normal manner of ministry still hundreds of years later; and didn't disappear until the time of Constanine? Instead, "the house church form was simply the natural result of their beliefs and values as modeled and initiated by [Jesus and the first] apostles."[11] (Brackets mine)

I will close this chapter with a very insightful – and scary – quote. "I fear for the future of authentic faith in our country. We live in a time when the common man in our country is thoroughly influenced by the current climate in which the cultural and educational elite propagate an anti-Christian message. We should take a look at what has happened in France and learn a lesson from it. In that country, Christianity has been *successfully attacked and marginalized* by these same groups *because those who professed belief were unable* [*or unwilling* due to the fear of man] to defend the faith from attack, even though its attackers' arguments are deeply flawed. We should be alarmed that instruction in authentic faith has been neglected, if not altogether eliminated, in our schools and universities, [and everywhere else imaginable]."[12] (Brackets and emphasis mine) It writes like today. It was written by William Wilberforce in 1797!

We really need to change the approach -- so we can be used to change the outcome.

CHAPTER NINE

WHAT IS A HOME GATHERING?

We have discussed the parameters of the house church principle as a whole and found that it is a general term for scripturally based small group ministry. Created by the Creator, established in full within the Kingdom of God, modeled clearly within the lifestyles recorded in the New Testament, it brings a methodology and a pattern of ministry to the table. A Home Gathering is a specific application of the house church dynamic. It offers a deeper, more refined, and more tangible usage of scripture and biblical principles. This chapter reflects that.

She came alone looking for help. She was probably in her late thirties, wearing a wedding ring, her husband was not with her. She was heavy of heart. For several years she had been experiencing chronic pain in her chest that would not go away. She had already been to her pastor and her doctor, the latter of whom sent her to a neurologist, who sent her to a psychologist, who sent her to a psychiatrist; all to no avail. What an ordeal. Having done what they could, no one had been able to sort it out or find a cause.

As is the usual format in a prayer ministry situation, while listening to her I was also listening to Holy Spirit for insight and instruction. She was wearing a locket around her neck that he pointed out to me. When I asked her about it, she opened it to reveal a picture of her son. When I asked about that, she opened up a bit and told the story. He was three when he was playing in the backyard one day and before she knew it, he had opened the gate, wandered through it, and was run over by a car. He died almost instantly. How overwhelmingly tragic. I spoke briefly to her about the dynamics of forgiveness and then asked her where she stood in that. I was prompted and was primarily interested in her forgiving herself. She assured me that she had worked through all that, including herself and the driver of the car. We moved on in dialog but Holy Spirit continued to draw me to the locket. Based on his insistence, I reintroduced conversation about her son and the afternoon of his death.

She was hesitant at first but after a moment, when I asked if we could pray for and over her, she consented. This was so amazingly powerful. Upon praying over her in the area of forgiveness and forgiving herself for the whole event, in the midst of trying to hold herself together, she broke down and began weeping and sobbing deeply. There were several of us gathered around her and one of the women began hugging her. She cried for some time in that woman's arms as the pain was released and Holy Spirit accomplished his healing work. She thought she had forgiven herself, but hadn't really; she just tried to hide the inner pain and tough it out. But now the pain was gone. Totally. And it never returned. She was free.

We never did pray about the pain. Holy Spirit knew the source of the pain, revealed it to another, directed the prayer ministry, and then in his love and compassion brought healing to one of his daughters. Just amazing. Word of Knowledge. Prophecy. Intercession. Prayer Ministry.

I share that story here because of its context. She was healed in the context of a Home Gathering, not at church or the pastor's office, or in any of the doctor's offices. It is not about the Gathering, but all about the *opportunity to engage* Holy Spirit that did not, or could not, happen in any other environment. This is God engaging with and using ordinary people to bring extraordinary supernatural things into the lives of his people, the people in his Kingdom. This is cutting edge ministry today. It is Holy Spirit breaking in. It is where he is heading. It may be uncharted water but this is who he is and where he is going. Again. It needs to be captured, learned, and lived out.

This reality is going on all over the world. It could be going on in your world...

I am using the term *home gathering* for some very intentional reasons. On the upside, both the words *home* and *gathering* speak volumes in the direction of a full definition giving way to a deep understanding of that to which we speak, that which we are studying and working toward, and that to which the Lord is calling us.

At the same time, there are some terms and phrases it just seems best to stay away from. This has to do with the baggage, or at least the perceived baggage, attached to them. For example, I rarely use the word "Christian" anymore. I am one, but I much prefer Follower-of-Jesus. This is because often, in our society, it seems that Christians are labeled as haters, as judgmental, or as fanatical with a very negative agenda. Whether these statements are true or not is not the point. It is *perceived* that way frequently. If I can stay away from that backlash, I usually will. I also choose to not use the word "church", at least most often. Stand on a street corner in your town and ask fifty people, "What is the first thing that comes to mind when I say the word church?" I'm quite confident their replies will not paint a pretty picture.

We are talking about house churches. This is a phrase that comes initially from Acts 2:46 and 5:42, where it says they met "from house to house." (NASB and NKJV) It is evidenced in many places throughout the rest of the New Testament, including Acts 2:2, 8:3, 10:22, 30, 12:12, 16:15, 32, 40, 20:20; Romans 16:5; 1 Corinthians 16:19; Colossians 4:15; Philemon 1:2, among others. It is a very reasonable label for the type of ministry that is reflected in the New Testament, and is now being fully established and built in the USA. Except for this: The house church movement is not new in this country. There are many well established entities that are strong, vibrant, and doing a great thing with and for God. Unfortunately, there are also a number of house churches that have been started by hurt and angry people. Having been, or perceived, rejected or shunned, they have started their own "church" and spend way too much time lambasting those whom they feel rejected them. Their focus is wrong, their motive is impure, they are more about themselves than others, and Jesus is often more of a side bar than the main focus. And it ends up being a "mini-church." That is to say that it looks and acts very similarly to a conventional church only on a smaller scale. It is still all about a certain personality, one who unfortunately is all too impressed with his or her opinions and voice.

Sorry to be so blunt; I am not intending to be judgmental, only observant. I just don't want people confused or uncertain about what God is working to build – and distinctly what he is not involved in building.

A Gathering does not have to be in a home. It is just the most convenient, warm, and uninhibited environment; a place where it is easy for people to let down, to be safe and at peace, and to open up to the greater things of life. The corner of a coffee shop or a lunch room, a board room or a conference room, or the back room of a restaurant can all work well, as can a hybrid situation involving people together in a home or coffee shop connecting with people online. The point is to gather in a location that is free from distraction where Jesus and Holy Spirit are not only welcome but are the focus.

I was invited into a church once to help them sort through the struggles they were having. In the midst of discussion with the senior pastor, I asked him about the principles and dynamics of allowing Holy Spirit to lead, on a Sunday morning or at any time throughout any week. His response was very sad – and unfortunately both common and revelatory: "Holy Spirit can do whatever he wants to do around here, he just has forty-five minutes to do it in." This was in reference to the approximate time spent in "worship" each Sunday morning. His statement made it perfectly clear just who was on the throne of his life and the church he was pastoring. Unfortunately, as we have already discussed, that position is the antithesis of God's heart and intention. In our context, it is not about times or locations or who is jockeying for position and control. It is all about *presence* and a *yielded heart to allow him his work.*

Chapter 10 will speak to this in fullness but it is appropriate to mention here. Why are we using the word *gathering*? The word means, "to cause to come together in one place or group; to assemble."[1] It is quite interesting that the origins of the word include the word *spouse.* Thus, the word speaks to the coming together of people relationally with depth. Powerful and significative word, actually.

In Scripture the word *gathering* is found quite often. It is a partial definition of another word, *sunago,* which we will talk about later. Both words together clearly and fully illuminate an amazingly rich understanding of depth in relationship, both vertically with the Trinity and horizontally with one another. It is community. Which means it is also unity, as the latter word is distinctly connected to the former. It is the real, open, honest, and integrous sharing and interacting of the depth of life together. What better word to use in the expression of life in Christ!

We intentionally do not use the phrase "small group." Although home gatherings are a type of small group, the phrase is too general and from that too vague. It does not hit the mark in expression or understanding. For similar reasons we do not use the phrase "cell group" or "cell church." The cell church movement is a wonderful happening as many are finding an expression of life with Christ they never knew. It is viable. The house church movement is more organic. The cells in a cell church are typically led by the senior leader of the church and his or her staff. The house church is led by those within it and are most often connected to a network of house churches in an interdependent manner. The difference might seem trite but it is not. A Home Gathering is learning how to lead -- by learning how to be led by Holy Spirit. The *main man* is Father God, his Son Jesus, and their equal Holy Spirit. This makes it unique and unlike a cell church and its cells.

Home Gatherings develop, "…when truly converted people stop living their lives for their own ends, and begin living a community life according to the values of the Kingdom of God, sharing their lives and resources with those [followers of Jesus] and the not-yet-[believers] around them."[2] (Brackets mine) Home Gatherings, "…are born of the conviction that we do not experience Jesus Christ and his Spirit only in sacred rooms dedicated for that express purpose, but we experience him in the midst of life. The organic house church is the deathbed of egoism and therefore, the birthplace of the church. True community starts where individualism ends."[3] Please understand that community life is not the same as a commune. "Community life pulverizes your old ego in the power of the Spirit of God, and rescues you from just living a miserable private life."[4] "I am working toward the day when communities of God's people, ordinary Christians whose lives regularly intersect, will accomplish most of the good we now depend on mental health professionals to provide. And they will do it by connecting with each other in ways that only the gospel, [the Kingdom of God,] makes possible… maybe the center of Christian community is connecting with a few."[5] (Brackets mine) "That man, and what he is doing and accomplishing in his living room, has saved me thousands of dollars in counseling money for my wife and my marriage."[6] These five quotes do a great job of capturing the heart and soul of Home Gathering ministry.

All of this being said, it is still more caught than taught. I don't know how many times I have heard the statement, "I had no idea," when someone experienced the sweetness and beauty of a Home Gathering for the first time.

A Home Gathering is comprised of ten to twenty folks meeting weekly in an environment that lends itself to a casual manner with warm, close, and healthy relationships centered in Jesus and his Kingdom. These groups are not intended to be highly structured. This does not mean they have no structure or directive. To the contrary, there is a specific structure that is to be clearly stated, taught on, and embraced. It is just designed in such a manner that it does not feel or appear to be highly structured.

Let me unpack that. A Home Gathering is intended to be low key and rather flat in terms of structure. The truth is that when any group of people gather "without structure" they have just established one! There is no such thing as no structure. If you pick a time to meet, or the hostess establishes an approximate time to eat, or you decide to pray before worshipping this week, you have just established structure. The fact is that in order for a group to pull off "warm and casual," the work behind the scenes is usually not casual and often not warm! There has to be intentionality and a specific and direct effort put forth to accomplish warm and casual. It may be like the clown in a bull riding contest. Although he looks casual, fun, and funny, he is none of that around a 2,000-pound angry bull! If he is not very intentional in every moment, he is in huge trouble!

In this model, every Gathering has a leader, male or female, who is competent and committed and flowing in the spiritual gifts of leadership and shepherding. There is also an assistant leader. "Two keys to this type of leadership are a strong person who knows how to *listen* and knows how to *accept and embrace* [people right where they are.]"[7] (Emphasis and brackets mine) These leaders are in a continual state of training and growing with this understanding: At the point in life that we quit learning we quit growing and we begin stagnating. The Kingdom of God is quite fluid and dynamic in its nature, and thus is ever advancing. Consequently, if we are not proactively moving forward with it, we are by default going backwards.

Every Gathering also has a host and/or hostess who is flowing in the spiritual gifts of hospitality, administration, serving, and helps. He or she, or they, is responsible for the administration of every Gathering, making sure that all are comfortable and well taken care of. This position is very important to the overall heartbeat of the group. There is a knack to making people feel comfortable, safe, and secure and when Holy Spirit is involved it is a beautiful thing.

There needs to be a facilitator as well. This person might be the leader, assistant leader or host, but not necessarily. The spiritual gift of administration is essential as the organization, development, and oversight of activities is their responsibility.

In this model, there are four elements that are essential and not optional. They are worship, teaching, prayer ministry, and fellowship, not necessarily in that order. And not necessarily in equal portions at every meeting. These elements are clearly seen in the New Testament model found in Acts 2:41-47. The concept is that over time these elements are in action and are balanced in time and thus in value. The scriptural basis for this, other than in Acts, is the Great Commandment found in Matthew 22:37-40.

Acts 2:41-47 is a primary and key passage outlining a healthy, encouraging, and appropriate life in the Kingdom. Four of those six verses speak to fellowship in its various dimensions. The NKJV translation of verse 46, where it says "from house to house," is the most accurate translation. They met corporately, primarily for intercessory type prayer and worship. They met in homes. They met over meals and had pointed discussions and debates -- that would translate today to interactive teachings. They prayed for and over each other -- that would translate today to prayer ministry. Worship, teaching, prayer, and fellowship.

Part of fellowship, of what we will come to know as *sunago*, has to do with the need for and value in recreation. Thus, built in to each Gathering, perhaps every four to six weeks, is an afternoon or evening of play, to be defined within the group.

Also, since the focus is to be one of Kingdom dynamics, at the outset, each Gathering works at outreach, and will work at walking out the Great Commission found in Matthew 28:18-20. This is expressed locally, nationally, and even internationally as the Lord leads. It is common that several groups choose to work together in developing their outreach activities. These are done every four to six to eight weeks, depending on the complexity of the outreach. Outreach is a Kingdom command; it is how God grows his Kingdom. A wonderful side affect is that this is also how each Gathering grows and multiplies.

The fact of the matter is that all types of small groups in America tend to stagnate and or die within six to twelve months. Part of the challenge is that most groups are aimed at ministering to the existent body rather than to the new or non-believers, and they are more designed as a maintenance ministry than a cutting-edge ministry. The bottom-line problem is one of commitment and a keen lack of *fresh blood*. New people help to keep any group more active, more energized. That's what the term fresh blood refers to.

It is imperative that these pursuits, these adventures be Spirit led and directed, and especially Spirit filled. This includes signs and wonders, power encounters, healings, deliverances, deep and significant heart changes authored and procured by the Spirit, prayer, and intercession. Coupled with faith to believe, all of this is essential. This is found within the reality of strong relationships and their results.

"A [Home Gathering] should provide a [safe and] loving environment which will encourage sharing of deep secrets of one's life [with no guilt, shame, criticism, or judgment.]"[8] (Brackets mine) Can you imagine feeling safe enough, and secure enough, and at peace enough to be able to open your heart wide open *without any fear of repercussion*? Is that even possible? Absolutely yes! I have been experiencing this for years, even decades. This is where and how we heal.

This brings up the thought of how to build a Home Gathering. Here is an exercise I once completed that helps to spell it out: "If you are going to start a [Home Gathering], tell us how you are going to do it. List all your planning, such as:

    a) where to get people,   **f)** how to expand,

b) how to proceed,	**g)** how to collect offerings,
c) when to meet,	**h)** how to use offerings,
d) where to meet,	**j)** where to get music, and
e) what's the focus,	**k)** anything else you can think of."[9]

a) The people, the initial leaders, will come [and already have come] from the relationships I have built within my Oikos, which is my circle of influence. As they begin to build, to draw people in from their oikos' they will be required to identify, recruit, and train the leader or leaders for the next round of Home Gatherings. Those leaders, in turn, will be required to do the same. All of this will happen within the relational dynamics that I have with them and they have with the next group, and on. This is how it will grow and expand. We call this being Born Pregnant **(f)**. Said another way, no new Home Gathering will start until the leader of the following Gathering has been identified and included into the existing entity. Thus, he or she will "learn the ropes" within a non-threatening, highly encouraging, learn-as-you-go environment **(k)**. There is nothing better than on-the-job training, in my opinion. There are times when this requirement is waived.

b) Each Home Gathering will proceed within a key and basic four-part structure. These Four Elements are Fellowship, Worship, Inter-active teaching, and Prayer Ministry. In no particular order and within no particular time frame. It may be that one week all we do is worship, or all we do is fellowship. It is just that in the overall, these four elements comprise the flow and go of the Home Gathering. It is highly encouraged that the Fellowship portion of this be centered around a meal, not just a snack.

(j) Worship is not and will not be just "music" or a three-song mini song service. It will be very intentionally an experience wherein the presence of the Lord is sensed, felt, and known by all. This is of the highest priority. It may be facilitated via guitar or keys; or via a cluster of worship songs from YouTube off someone's iPad; or some creative combination. With regularity there will be times when multiple Home Gatherings will come together for a more corporate worship experience, most often with the other three Elements included.

c) Our preferred and default time to meet will be on Fridays, in the home of the Leader or Host, preferably the latter, **(d)** late afternoon and into the evening. Most often the time together will start with a meal, including communion. **(k)** This is fully subject to the preference of each Home Gathering and may vary or shift over time. Often, times together will naturally expand to more than once per week as *Out There* and *Things to do Together,* two of the components of each Home Gathering, develop. **(k)**

e) The focus will be life in Christ in the lives of those involved. This in the many variants found within the principles and tangible realities of a deep, experiential, transferable life in Christ, from Scripture, and from his Spirit. It will be relational, personal, familial, and communal in nature, in the context of self, neighbor, and beyond, and on as the Lord leads.

g) **(h)** All of these associations and the expansions therein do and will fall under and within the cover of an already existent 501(c)3 non-profit church corporation. All monies will be collected at the Home Gathering level, brought into the Corporation, and redistributed according to need and planned expenditures; each Home Gathering having the authority to plan its own. As there is very little overhead, most all monies will be used in a manner of ministry. This will include community *Out There* ministry endeavors, Home Gathering Community activities, Benevolence ministry, *Things We Do Together* activities, Offerings to other ministries, and on.

And, in the context of *how* to build, comes the understanding of *what* a Home Gathering is based on. Our Philosophy of Ministry regarding Home Gatherings is as follows:

We believe Home Gatherings are designed and intended, by God, via the Scriptures, to be a strong, viable, and critical part of the whole of life in the follower-of-Jesus experience, to the extent wherein they carry a higher share of value than any or all corporate encounters.

We believe it is within this environment where the fullness of relationship, which is of such vital importance in the Kingdom and to the heart of God, is to be found, nurtured, and developed to its fullness. Hence, we will continually work toward the goal of involving all people and all Home Gatherings of all types into the completeness of small group dynamics. Herein will be taught, modeled, discovered, and maintained depth and true meaning of interpersonal relationships, with our Lord and one another. From this will come true community. (Acts 2:42-44)

We believe this includes, but is not limited to, the healthy and rich development and application of the concepts and principles given by God for "the whole measure of the fullness of Christ" in our lives. (Ephesians 4:12) Herein is found the purposes of Home Gatherings, which are as follows:

1. To make disciples, "determined learners." (Matthew 28:18-20)

2. To build the body of believers to the place of unity and community. (Genesis 48:4; Acts 2:42-44, 4:32-35; Ephesians 2:22, 4:12,13)
3. To "mature the saints for the works of service" to and for their Lord. (Ephesians 4:13)
4. To develop and enhance the vertical and horizontal relationships created, ordained and mandated by God as part and parcel of his Kingdom. (Matthew 22:37-40)
5. To create and establish an environment wherein people can identify and grow in spiritual gifts and thus fulfill their call in the Kingdom. (Ephesians 4:13)
6. To perpetrate, advance and multiply Home Gatherings that others may also gain and grow in Christ.
7. To advance the Kingdom of God throughout the whole world. (Matthew 28:18-20)

We believe these ongoing encounters are to be pursued and fully engaged by all within the body of believers to the extent wherein they become a mindset and a lifestyle.

It is our intent as a body of believers to subscribe to, and follow through with, the position found within these statements to their fullness so as to bring to fruition a model of ministry that is fully consistent with, and reflective of, the one found within the New Testament.

In the interest of drawing all of this together, the following phrases must be understood and embraced by all, not just leaders. This contributes to ownership. The more people see and understand, the more involved they want to be. These are the nuts and bolts of Home Gathering life:

Who are we, and what are we working toward:

- Continuous training and equipping

- Living, breathing, praying, portraying healthy biblical life principles
- Relationship, relationship, relationship
- Humility, humility, humility, humility
- Kingdom, Kingdom, Kingdom
- Outreach oriented
- Higher levels of commitment
- Lower levels of expectation
- Prayer as a high priority
- Worship as the highest priority
- Driven by a cause, not a personality – that is Jesus and his Kingdom
- Nurturing a gentle and generous lifestyle

Where do we gather:

- Homes
- Break rooms
- Board rooms
- Conference rooms
- Coffee shops
- Restaurants
- Online
- Hybrid: part in person, part online

When do we gather:

- At various times throughout the week, whenever it fits

A Home Gathering is designed and intended to facilitate life in Christ to its fullest possibilities. It is structured in such a way so as to meet the primary needs in peoples lives within the context of strong and healthy community. These needs include, but are not limited to:

- "People need to become lovers of God. (John 13:34-35)
- People need a family; they need to become a family. (Ephesians 4:15-16; Romans 12:4; 1 Corinthians 12:12-13, 26-27)
- People need a place to discover and develop spiritual gifts. (Romans 12:4-10; 1Corinthians 12:14; Ephesians 4:11-18)
- People need a place to learn to pray. (1 Corinthians 14:15; James 5:16; 1 Timothy 2:1; 1 Thessalonians 3:10)
- People need a place to learn to praise and worship God. (Luke 24:52-53; 1 Peter 2:9)
- People need a place to discover their ministry; a safe place for trial and error, for growth. (1 Peter 4:11)"[10]

CHAPTER TEN

SUNAGO: THE HEART OF IT ALL

O ver the course of a lifetime of study and research into the heart of God and his Word, his ways and means, his intents and purposes, there are certain words and passages, and their meanings, that stand above the rest. The Greek word *sunago* is one such word.

This word, which reveals the heart of the matter, which exposes and illuminates the revelation of the heart of God, which brings *the working definition of the Kingdom of God* to the forefront, is the key word. This may seem overstated, but it is not.

Jesus said in Matthew 12:30, "He who is not with me is against me, and he who does not *gather* with me scatters." In Matthew 18:20 he said, "For where two or three have *gathered* in my name, I am there in their midst." And then in 25:35 he said, "For... I was a stranger and you *invited* me in..." All three of these highlighted words are the word *sunago*.

I first encountered the word *sunago* through a study I initiated on the word *community,* to which we are all called. The root word of community is "common" or "shared by all." In Greek it is *koinos.* You have probably heard the word *koinonia,* which translates as fellowship or sometimes friendship. It comes from *koinos. Koinos* comes from another Greek word which is *sun,* and is pronounced "soon." *Sun* means "union" or "together" and is the first half of our word.[1] The second half of the word is *ago* and is pronounced "ah'-go." It means to lead or to bring. Sun-ag'-o. Draw the two words together and its basic meaning is "to lead together or to bring together or to bring to union."[2]

You can see that *koinonia* is part of what I'm getting at but is not the whole of it. The word *sunago* reflects the full concept and meaning of community. We are created by Community for community. By that I mean that the Triune God is community; they are one and have all things in common. Within that actuality, they created us in their image. We are intended for community, we thrive in community, and we experience serious struggle outside community.

The principles of community and their practical applications are vitally important and valuable in our relationship with God. He is quite emphatic about it. For example:

- Our relationship with the Triune Godhead, and their relationship with each other is about community. (John 17)
- The whole of the 1 Corinthian letter is about community. 1 Corinthians 3 and on through the rest of the book addresses the Corinthian people and hinges from a discourse on division, which is the opposite of unity. And unity is at the heart of community.
- The gifts of the Spirit operate within community. They are all expressed within a plural context. (Ephesians 4:8 and 1 Corinthians 11:17-18)
- The armor of God is enhanced and fully developed within community. Ephesians 6:12 is plural and is in the context of the second half of the book, which starts in chapter 4 with the phrase, "I urge you…," which is plural.
- The fruits of the Spirit are expressed and exercised within community. Galatians 5:7, 11, 13, 16, and 24 are all plural.
- Spiritual warfare only bears fruit within community. Ephesians 6:10 and 2 Corinthians 10:3-5 are all plural.
- The call to intercession is found in plural form, it is designed to be community. The watchmen on the walls in Isaiah

62:6 were not working solo. Remember that the Jews were keen on community. Even in the task of watching, which is indicative of intercession, they often worked in teams as some of the towers built had rooms attached for sharing food or for sleeping while another stood watch.

This having been said, the breadth and depth of community is best defined, seen, and understood by way of *sunago*.

The various ways in which the word is translated into English include, "to collect, to convene, to accompany, assemble, bestow, come together, gather together, gather, lead into, invite, and take in."[3] It is interesting and revelatory to see that there are primarily three Greek words that indicate a closeness. They are *meta,* which means "with" or "to accompany," *para,* which means "near," and *sunago,* which is the closest, and from that the most intimate word.[4]

Sunago is used fifty-nine times in the New Testament (NIV) in these ways:

"gathered, gather, gathered together, gathering, met, assembled, got together, met together, bring together, called together, came together, come together, invite in, and caught."[5] It is also interesting that in all instances the word comes forth as a participle, as an action, as an energy expended. A participle is a noun used as a verb for expression and poignancy. That means it is not a casual word but one of importance and impact. Along with others, Jesus is using the word as a verb, an action word, to bring emphasis and added value.

An excellent example of this can be accurately illustrated within our American history in the phenomenon of some of the pioneers travelling west and their practice of circling the covered wagons at the end of the day. What were they doing? Preparing and eating meals together. Encouraging each other over the events and struggles of the day. Sharing life. Protecting each other from the elements: wild animals, the weather, the bad guys. Creating an environment where all were safe, covered, and looked after. Engaging in interpersonal relationships. Think about it: If we are standing in a circle, I can see behind you, and you me. I have your back, and you mine. This was one of the reasons to form the wagons in a circle. All of this excellently tells the story of *sunago*.

Further research expands the depth of the meaning in this way: "To gather things in such as fish of every kind, crops of the field, and sheep; to join with someone in gathering, to invite or receive a guest, to reconcile, to muster, to bring or call together, or to gather a number of persons."[6] And then, "to take into one's house, meaning to give hospitality and protection."[7] Two different derivatives add more insight: *episunago* means "to gather together in one place," and *sunathleo* means "to wrestle in company with; to seek jointly; to struggle in company with."[8] All of this data adds up to a very deep and broad understanding of our word. (Don't miss this: It is highly evidenced that there is the flavor of healthy relational depth within the parameters of reconciliation and its natural outcome of restoration found in *sunago*. And both of these are the Father's business.)

Sunago is life in Christ together. It captures in fullness the complete dynamics of community. Wrestling and struggling through together is only found in a world of selflessness, of "...esteeming others more highly than self." (Philippians 2:3, paraphrase mine) To gather together in one place, with one heart, with one intention reflects community, and the Triune God is community. *Sunago* reflects God and his heart. And from there, his Kingdom. Powerful.

A rich expression of this is found in Philippians 1:27d, "...that [y'all] stand firm in one spirit, contending as one man for the faith of the gospel..." The NASB says it this way: "...that [y'all] are standing firm in one spirit, with one mind striving together for the faith of the gospel..." And the AMP says, "...that [y'all] are standing firm in united spirit and purpose, striving side by side and contending with a single mind for the faith of the glad tidings." (Brackets mine) Any way you read it, it is amazing and quite powerful.

This is how we have been created! It is the Father's heart

that we live fully in the manner in which we have been created.

The deeper history of our word is amazing. Please read what follows with the understanding that just like with a name, a word carries with it a history and a depth of meaning that gives it weight and worth. The history brings flavor and a richer meaning to the word or words. One can see the intricacies and nuances. Think of how all the different ingredients, even in small amount, affect the overall flavor of a great soup or stew.

The Classical Greek definition of the word is: "The collecting or bringing together of things such as books, letters, possessions, fruit, troops, or people." Its "…most specialized and clear meaning is this: In the activities of the guilds; for the regular, mostly festive assembly, linked with a meal and sacrifice"[9] "Guilds" would be the groups, clans, families, or clusters of people. This is Home Gatherings! "Regular" would equate to the weekly or routine meetings. "Mostly festive" has all to do with the underlying tone or mood. This is living in the fruits of the Kingdom. And "a meal and sacrifice" are clearly referencing fellowship and worship and prayer. This is the history behind who and what we are about today, the history of *sunago* -- and Home Gatherings!

A sidebar: The Fruits of the Kingdom include:

- The Fruits of the Spirit
- The Beatitudes
- The detailed principles found in Acts 2:41-47, especially those in verses 42-44 which are commitment and community surrounding signs and wonders
- The applied principles of *Sunago*
- A life based around the Gifts of the Spirit, which are truly the tools provided for the job, which bring healings and miracles -- and salvations in abundance. And fulfillment for those being used by Holy Spirit in this context.

- This is where he wants us to live! This is our reason for being. This is where, "we live and move and have our being." (Acts 17:28)

In the Septuagint, *sunago* is used for the Hebrew word *edah*. "In the earliest strata of the Old Testament, [this word] stands primarily for the summons to war of all men capable of bearing arms." Also, "The people which Yahweh has summoned." And "The people gathered before the tent of meeting. This *edah* is divided up into tribes, clans and families, led by elders, heads and princes."[10] (Brackets mine)

The word expresses a concept of corporate-ness, in which the stress falls "not on the total of individuals, on the crowd, but in *the unity of the fellowship*." Then, "The word in practice covers the people *as a community* in all its functions, of which even the most secular was not without some connection with the law and the sanctuary." And "It is not bound to a particular land or a particular place."[11] (Emphasis mine)

"The *edah* is the unambiguous and permanent term for the covenant community as a whole. [It] is the permanent community into which one was born [i.e., born again] and in which one possessed certain rights and responsibilities in an exactly determined and defined measure." In this there is a clear and distinct "dynamic of the summons to the community." Thus, the meaning, "congregation of unity."[12] (Brackets mine) I think that says it all.

Since the word *gather* or *gathering* is found so often within the concept and principles of *sunago*, and *sunago* is so very important, it seems reasonable to label and call all that we build as "Gatherings" and "Home Gatherings."

To close this chapter, I taught a class that included the principle of *sunago*. I asked my students to define it in their own words. Here are some of their responses:

- A deep sense of intimate relationship with others, not like koinonia, but a deeper sense of relationship.
- To have relationship with, to build up, to edify, to stand together in unity and to strengthen. A time of communion, community, and support.
- The gathering together of the body in one.
- A group of believers in a community of family and unity.
- God's people gathering together on purpose.
- An intimate community of relationship, care, and trust.
- A community of believers in Christ with a single purpose.
- A community of like-minded and like-hearted individuals serving each other for the greater purpose.
- A community lifestyle where all are at work together functioning as one.

Sunago, the *heart of it all* and the *working definition of the Kingdom of God.*

PART THREE

THE PRACTICS: THIS IS WHERE WE LIVE!

CHAPTER ELEVEN

CULTIVATING AN
ARENA OF TRUST

N
ow we are switching gears and moving into the practical application of what we have been discussing. We are starting with the principle of trust.

Trust. Heavy word. Huge ramifications found within it. Trust and mistrust are core to everyone's heart and life, and thus very meaningful. Trust is defined as, "Reliance on the integrity, strength, ability, and surety of a person; confidence. Confident expectation of something; hope. To have trust or confidence in; to rely or depend on. Reliance on and confidence in the truth, worth, reliability of a person; faith."[1] Several different Greek words come into English as trust and mean, "To expect or confide: have hope, trust. To anticipate; expectation or confidence: faith, hope. To entrust. To rely (by inward certainty). To experience reliance: confidence, trust."[2] Powerful word in either direction, in trust or mistrust.

I'm addressing this first because it is of the utmost importance. It is essential. Trust is a close brother, I would suggest a twin brother, to faith. Relationships are built on trust, that is trust established, nurtured, and developed. Intentionally. With honesty, integrity, and sincerity. Face-to-face, heart-to-heart type trust. That is what works in the healthy building of any relationship, certainly of any people-oriented ministry.

That having been said, without the trust, without the genuine relationships, without the honesty and integrity found within trust – well, good luck because it will not last. One of my sons-in-law has said of me that, "I find you painfully honest!" I take that as a compliment. I also take that as a challenge. My Lord has made it perfectly clear to me, down through time, that I am to carry myself in a forthright manner, with honesty and integrity, transparency and vulnerability, in kindness and gentleness. This is what builds trust in me in the hearts of those around me.

Many years ago, a pastor friend of mine called me and asked if we could get some coffee together. He said, "I know you to be a forthright man of God and I need some of that right now." This little story is not about me, then or now. I just think we all need a whole lot of forthrightness right now!

"I just slapped my son," was a text I received one day. How was that person able to be so vulnerable, especially with someone not in their own family? I built trust. I built a real, tangible arena of safety and security, with stability, with a clear understanding of my agenda, which is no agenda. Except to help. To support. To come under and build up. To stand alongside. That mom reached out to me in the context of a strong trust relationship because she knew she had overreacted and needed some help. Which she received, by the way, and worked things out with her son.

On another occasion, I met with a couple from our Home Gathering. After listening to the wife share some of the challenges she was having regarding her husband and their teenage son, it was his turn. Before he began his response, I asked him, "How are you feeling right now?" In the broader context of marriage counseling, I have learned to expect an answer that has something to do with his agitation over being exposed and not being respected, or some other seemingly defensively postured statement. Instead, his response was simply, "I am at peace. I feel at peace right now. I feel comfortable." Where did that come from? From the atmosphere of trust that I established and had nurtured with them over time. Trust.

Want to plant a church? Want to grow a Home Gathering, or a cluster of Home Gatherings? Win their trust. Win it with humility. Win it with a demonstrated brokenness that exposes your heart — and its lack of agenda. For example, it has been said that a woman can determine the motive of a man within ten seconds of initial contact. (I know a number of women who adamantly disagree with this statement. They say it is accomplished within five seconds!) If he has an agenda, she will sniff it out in a heartbeat. She may not know just exactly what his agenda is, but she will know whether the man's intentions are pure or upright or not almost instantly. Honesty, integrity, sincerity, and transparency are huge elements in this life, especially in this walk with Jesus. In this assignment of advancing the Kingdom of God, they are crucial.

Recognize that Father has no problem exposing the inherent weaknesses found within the lives of those he talks about and uses. Moses and Abraham, Joseph and David, Samuel and Elijah, Jonah, Paul and Timothy. The list goes on. He did not do this to embarrass them — even though it may have. He did this to refine and grow them, to build character in their souls. And he did this to set for us an example of how to live this life. Is it any different for you and me? So, why not just flow with his work in your heart? And let others see that work. Because then it is easy for them to follow suit. Your integrity, your transparency, builds trust — and establishes the arena of same through which Holy Spirit can then flow without restriction.

Yes, build the church. Yes, build the master plan. Yes, market it well if you must. But be genuine and humble, know who you are and who you are not and be in shalom there. Be real. Build true, honest, strong relationships. One at a time, over time. With integrity and intentionality.

I once was invited into a group of business men and women to offer some counsel and advice regarding my perspectives and dynamics on how to operate a successful business. What transpired had nothing to do with strategies or tactics. It became a charge to them, a commissioning actually. This is a synopsis of what was spoken:

- Be true to you
- Be truly the person you are – in Christ
- Walk fully in the knowledge of who you are
- Which includes the knowledge of who you are not
- Walk in the full understanding that you truly are
    child to the King
    brother or sister to the Christ
    and your personal trainer is Holy Spirit
- Live Micah 6:8, which says to walk humbly, do justly, and love mercy
- Walk in humility and in full adoration for and toward your God
- Walk in the humble confidence given you by your God, found in a right relationship with him
- See that your business or ministry is an extension, a manifestation of you
- Know that you are not all things to all people – that position has been taken!

In other words:

- Walk in confidence – his in you
- Don't be the answer man; just be you
- Enhance your strengths
- Be aware of your weaknesses
- Learn the value of delegation
- Learn and apply just how and when to say no.

All of this is how you build trust. All of this is applicable in any business, in any family, and in any ministry. The arena of trust is paramount. There are other arenas that must also be constructed. I will not go into them here except to mention a few of them. Essential are the arenas of servanthood, of acceptance and patience, and of excellence. Of great significance is the arena of presence; just be present without having to speak or bring an answer.

One more thought to end this chapter. Research has proven that a full eighty-five percent of people who come to Jesus do that through a friend. Not a pastor or a church service. Not some crusade or evangelical meeting. If that friendship is not based on and built within an arena of trust, that encounter with Jesus will never happen. Think about that.

CHAPTER TWELVE

THE FOUR ELEMENTS

aving highlighted the primary value of building an arena of trust, we now move on to the primary sphere of activity, that being what I call the *four elements* of ministry.

An element is defined as, "a natural habitat, sphere of activity, environment, etc.; an atmospheric agency or force."[1] I like that word because its definition fits so very well into the Home Gathering and Sunago understanding. A Gathering is truly an atmospheric agency and force.

I have mentioned that we led our first small group when I was only six months old in the Lord. We created our first small group a couple years later. We knew nothing! We knew Jesus and we knew some of the joy found in relationships at a certain level of depth. Other than that, we were fish out of water. I quickly found out that no one else around me knew anything either. The Lord placed us into the middle of a style of ministry that was completely foreign to us. He did not teach me how to swim first; he just threw me in the lake! Oh, and then stood by to make sure I didn't drown!

I had been taught – and to this day will vehemently defend – that the source to seek when needing help, when needing to learn, grow, or adjust was the Word. It is the Living Word, and when coupled with Holy Spirit, is the spring, the birthplace, the unending river of all things wise and revelatory.

The first church was primarily comprised of people living life together. Since that is recorded in the Word, that is where I went to gain at least some semblance of how to do small group ministry.

And that is where I have been going ever since. It didn't take too long to land in Acts 2:42-47, which is a primary and key passage outlining a healthy and appropriate life in the Kingdom, both at large and by way of small group ministry. From here the Lord has revealed so much about the hows and whats of this style of ministry. The verses read:

> "42They devoted themselves to the apostles' teaching and to the fellowship, to the breaking of bread and to prayer. 43Everyone was filled with awe, and many wonders and miraculous signs were done by the apostles. 44All the believers were together and had everything in common. 45Selling their possessions and goods, they gave to anyone as he had need. 46Everyday they continued to meet together in the temple courts. They broke bread in their homes and ate together with glad and sincere hearts, 47praising God and enjoying the favor of all the people. And the Lord added to their number daily those who were being saved."

Almost every time I read or deeply study this passage I am affected by the presence of Holy Spirit and impacted by the significance of the presence and power expressed therein. I wonder what would happen if you just took a few minutes and settled into re-reading it two or three times, slowly, allowing the Lord to speak to your heart.

When you add the dynamic, the *dynamis*, which is the Greek word for "power when expressed by God,"[2] of verse 41 to the mix it becomes almost overwhelming. "Those who accepted his message were baptized, and about three thousand were added to their number that day." Try to imagine that. This is not Peter impressing people while waxing eloquent with some three-part sermon polished to the max. This is the power, presence, and conviction of Holy Spirit drawing "all men" (Acts 22:15) to himself. "Of all descriptions of Christian churches in the New Testament, this first church planted in Jerusalem on the Day of Pentecost is the one a great many today would choose to imitate if they could."[3]

If they could. I would add to that, *if they would*. We have entered into a season where if a group of people will but press in, seek, and pursue the Lord in this realm they will begin to see the manifestations of Holy Spirit. Which we all need and are hungry for to bring revival, renewal, and transformation.

It was through that passage of scripture that I first began to understand the *four elements* that comprise what we do together every week and the value and resultant depth of life, in him and with each other, found therein. They are *teaching, fellowship, prayer ministry*, and *worship*.

Teaching is a critical part of growing in Christ. Teaching with excellence helps people grow into excellence. It is worth the effort to learn how to teach in a manner that stirs the hearts of others to that place where actual growth happens. As Holy Spirit is the Counselor and Guide (John 16:13), we do well to learn how to allow him to lead. I believe it to be imperative that all teachings be formatted into an interactive teaching model. The following chapter details this model. Within this style of teaching, people get an opportunity to partake and contribute. One of the biggest challenges in the western world of small group ministry is that often the leader feels the need to preach, to offer up a monologue. This most often turns the small group into a mini-church centered on one. Within the interactive teaching model, the door is opened for Holy Spirit to direct traffic. When that happens, people grow.

Fellowship is where relationships develop and deepen. This is friendship, fun, food, and frolic. This is sharing in the positive areas of life. It is the giving and receiving of encouragements and affirmations in the midst of upbeat activities as simple as sharing time over coffee, or as complex as creating a neighborhood community service outreach. We are created for community; we need people.

Fellowship, if intentionally developed, fulfills that need; it builds lasting friendships.

There is another dimension found within the element of fellowship. As was discussed in an earlier chapter, the practical and pointed dynamic of sunago is intended to be found here. Where fellowship could be defined with the Greek word *koinonia*, which basically means friendship, fellowship in this context is much better exercised on the level of sunago. Rich, deep, lifelong, personal relationships with Christ at the center is the objective.

Also to be considered within the element of fellowship are two additional matters: food and communion. We sweet-toothed Americans tend to go for the cookies and donuts with our coffee after the more formal times of the evening are over. You will hear no complaints about that pattern from me! There are some viable alternatives. The first church practiced a different model. Their times of fellowship most often included a meal and would start the time together. This is a great way to get to know each other even better, and it helps newcomers to feel more included. Their expression of communion was also not a wafer and a dollop of grape juice. They took the time to bring remembrance in the context of the meal; it was literally a communion meal every time they met.

Prayer Ministry is all about listening to the needs of people while at the same time listening to the communications, instructions, and directions of Holy Spirit and flowing accordingly -- by faith and through prayer and prophetic communication. It is important to understand that most often this does not come naturally – it is a learned behavior. I believe it is one of the most fluent, effective, and powerful means of ministry, from God to mankind. I also believe it is seriously misunderstood and grossly under used. Watch and see what will happen amongst you if you determine to focus and grow in this area.

Worship speaks to an opportunity to get up close and personal with the Triune God. It is often within the context of music, but does not have to be. Our command is to worship him in Spirit and truth.

(John 4:23-24) His demand is that we worship him with all of our heart, mind, soul, and strength. (Luke 10:27) He is first. Worship can help us to align with that, to emphasize that, to come into full alignment with him and his heart. It is critical in the context of the deep and rich relationship we have been talking about. We do well to maintain a high priority toward it. CD, Mp3, YouTube, guitar, keyboard, even a cappello, can all be a means to this end. Being intentionally redundant, don't neglect or discount this element. It is way more significant than it is commonly given credit to. True worship breeds true intimacy with the Lord your God.

These *four elements* need be exercised in no particular order, and not necessarily in equal portions at every meeting. The concept is that over the long haul these elements are in action and are balanced in time and thus in value. Perhaps one evening the entire time would be spent in worship, or in prayer ministry. Another time there might be an important topic that everyone wants to dig into and the whole evening simply evolves into that. The point is not to use a stop watch and restrict each element to thirty minutes in a two-hour format. The point is that over time a balance will be found amongst the four. They all interlock with each other. They feed and build on one another. They complement and enhance one another.

There is more insight from Acts 2:42-47 to consider, specifically verses 42-44. It is a God-given principle that is well worth contemplating and embracing. In verse 42 we see devotion: "They *devoted* themselves to teaching and fellowship…" The word means, "zealous or ardent in attachment, loyalty."[4] The idea of *commitment* comes to mind, which can mean, "dedication, allegiance, obligation."[5] This was anything but casual. This was a way of life, the manner in which they went about the business of living. It was an obligation, but of a voluntary nature. They didn't have to work at or stress about it because of the fulfillment that came from it. Could we live there?

Then in verse 44 we find *unity* and *community*. There is unity in community and it was fully evidenced here. They, "were together and had everything in common." This does not mean they lived in a communal type environment. This means they lived within the directives of "esteeming others more highly than yourself" and "deferring to the other." (Philippians 2:3) They all carried an attitude of caring and helping, of investing in one another as needed.

So, we have commitment to the cause coupled with a strong, caring community. And what do we find between these, in verse 43? The power and presence of Holy Spirit bringing awe and amazement: "Everyone was filled with awe, and many wonders and miraculous signs were done..." If we will follow the Lord's lead and get serious about living the lifestyle we have been invited into, we will personally experience signs and wonders and even be used as a vessel through which he flows to bring them to others. I want that! You?

CHAPTER THIRTEEN

THE HOW-TO OF
INTERACTIVE TEACHING

O ne of the underlying principles of this style of ministry is this: no bleachers, no spectators. Involving people is vital. It is how they grow, how they heal, and how they fall more in love with their Lord. It is how they become safer and more secure in their soul, in their life. It is how they develop that confidence that comes from God's heart to theirs – which comes no other way. All of this contributes to and is enhanced by interactive teaching.

There are five steps in the process of developing an interactive teaching:

1. Discover: Find the subject matter.
2. Study: Engage the subject matter.
3. Seek: Ask questions of the text, the subject matter.
4. Receive: Obtain the answers.
5. Build: Structure the teaching.

Follow these steps diligently to develop interactive teachings. All of this must be accomplished by following the Lord's lead. Within an attitude of prayer and study, allow Holy Spirit to direct your path in terms of what he wants taught and discussed. It is in that context that you are looking for the (1) discovery of the subject matter. Once this has been determined, narrow your study; this is (2) engaging the subject matter. This step is critical as the entirety of the discussion will center around your findings. As you are studying, invite Holy Spirit to lead you deep into the text.

Here is where you (3) ask questions of the text to get to the heart of the matter. What is the Lord's agenda, what is he saying, what does he want imparted in the story and to the reader? What, if any, is the kickback or resistance and why? What are the others within the story thinking and why? How are they reacting and what does that say? There are a multitude of questions to be asked. The more you do this the more refined you become in the asking. That is because you are learning to hear Holy Spirit. He is the Teacher teaching you how to teach!

Having asked questions, now seek to (4) obtain answers. Prayer and meditation are very important here. Don't just answer the question the way you think it ought to be answered. Research. Dig. Gain the Lord's answers; gain his wisdom and understanding, and seek his revelation. This is what we are all hungering and thirsting for!

When you have the answers, go back to him and ask for the applications. (5) Structure the teaching around that. Keep the teaching in bite-size pieces. And resist the temptation to go too long or too far in one setting. I suggest using bullet points to identify the questions and answers.

Take this to the interactive discussion, asking the questions, looking for and drawing the answers from the group. *Do not bring the answer!* Draw it from the others. This is the most critical point. Let Holy Spirit flow, orchestrate, and choreograph. Wait on him. Some silence is not at all a negative. In fact, it can actually lend itself to the ease and comfort of the time together. Relax.

Learn the techniques of directing and re-directing to keep the flow within the parameters of the subject. Ask the right question and you can be quiet for twenty minutes, needing only to direct traffic so as to keep the flow of dialogue on track and on point. Good leaders learn and operate here, thus giving their followers opportunity to think and process for themselves - and grow. And even more importantly, connect with the Teacher, Holy Spirit. This will keep things right and true and not on some tangent or incorrect thought line.

Learn to draw everyone into the discussion. Use phrases like, "That's good. What does someone else have to offer?" "What do you think about that, Joe?" "Okay. Perhaps. Does someone else want to add to that?" "Let's be careful not to go down a rabbit trail here. We might fall into a rabbit hole!" Be careful not to over-draw people. Making someone uncomfortable by forcing them into the center of attention will make everyone uneasy. And it does not build trust, in that person or anyone in the group. In the early stages of development "Joe" needs to be your spouse or your assistant leader, and they need to know ahead of time your intention to potentially draw them in.

You are the leader. So, lead. Just emphatically resist the temptation to answer your own questions! Perhaps the question will need to be rephrased, but never answered by you. When answers begin to come, move the discussion around the room. Be sensitive to those who are shy or skittish. Don't force or push anyone into verbalizing, they will engage when they are ready.

Don't push to get the entire teaching delivered within a specific time frame. If time is up, keep the rest for next week, or another time. On the other hand, if the discussion runs short of the anticipated time frame, do not fill with fluff. Simply move on to whatever is next on the evening schedule. If it becomes obvious that the questions are not being answered, that the group is not engaging the subject, you may have to reconsider either the value of the subject or the manner in which you are asking. A question needs to be clear, concise, and not too complex. Offer small bites; they are easier to chew.

Again, you are the leader. So, lead. Just remember that true leadership is servant leadership.

It. Cannot. Ever. Be. About. You.

It. Must. Always. Be. About. Jesus. And others.

Healthy and effective leadership must be sacrificial leadership; you are the sacrifice.

Realize that when people are given the opportunity to speak, to share in the discussion, it is very edifying to them. It helps them to feel valued and valuable. Unless the leader is maneuvering people for his own gain, when this happens, it is genuine and that person will grow from the experience. And over time, will take on a legitimate level of ownership in the group, perhaps becoming your next leader.

I find it best to create series of subject matter. People gain and go deeper from some repetition. When you hear them saying things they have learned from the discussions, you are succeeding. When those things have come from someone other than you, that means they are learning from each other and you are really succeeding! Within this realm of teaching, is the tangible reality of Matthew 18:20, which says, "For where two or three are gathered together in my name, I am there in their midst." When Holy Spirit is invited in, he shows up. And when he is given his rightful place as Lord, he leads. And things happen.

I once created a thirty-nine-week class that met every Sunday evening for three-plus hours. With homework. The intention was to take a group of adults as deep into the heart of Jesus as was possible within that nine-month time frame. There was Scripture to read and study. There were books to read and papers to write. There were two different retreats. There were outreach and service projects. It was brutal! And everyone rose to the occasion. It was a wonderful time with many wonderful testimonies and lifelong friendships developed. The best part was seeing them grow deeper in their relationship with their Lord.

One of the primary points of structure was that we had small group ministry for about forty-five minutes within the evening every week. This was to expose people to that style of ministry. And to build trust. Every week I had everyone line up and I counted out one through five down the line. That created five groups with a variety of numbers of people. I mixed it up so the net result was that each group was different each week. They had to pick the leader for the group for that week amongst themselves.

These people mostly did not know each other. They were much more comfortable sitting and listening to me than being required into engaging and interacting with others. Which was exactly my point. It is called transformational leadership. It is taking people where they need to go – even and especially if they don't want to. Oh, don't blame me. It was not my idea. Whose idea do you suppose it was? They were forced out of their comfort zones, and into developing and demonstrating acceptance, tolerance, and patience. They were forced into leading and following. From that, they built trust. Rich and deep trust that strengthened them all, personally and collectively.

It was a bit of an experiment. It was risky. It could have failed miserably, but it didn't. Holy Spirit was in it. It bloomed and grew and prospered. It was amazing. Why am I sharing this story? All this equates to the maturing of the person and the group at large. This is the maturing of the saints talked about in Ephesians 4:13.

We cannot become *what* we need to be, *what* our Lord is building us to be, by remaining *what* we are.

But of more importance, we cannot become *who* we need to be, *who* our Lord is building us to be, by remaining *who* we are.

Be patient… and wait… and you will see, oh, so much of the Lord's glory!

CHAPTER FOURTEEN

THE WHAT'S AND WHY'S OF SPIRITUAL GIFTS

"No local [Home Gathering] will be what it <u>could</u> *be,*
what Jesus prayed it <u>should</u> *be,*
what Holy Spirit gifted and empowered it <u>to</u> *be,*
until it understands and is fluid in the use of spiritual gifts."[1]
(Emphasis and brackets mine)

"A Christian who does not have a ministry based on his or her use
of spiritual gifts is a contradiction in terms."[2]

"Earnestly desire spiritual gifts, especially the gift of prophecy.
Be eager to prophesy, and do not forbid speaking in tongues."
(1 Corinthians 14:1, 39)

"Now about spiritual gifts, brothers and sisters,
I do not want you to be ignorant."
(1 Corinthians 12:1)

"We have different [spiritual] gifts, according to the grace given us."
(Romans 12:6a. Brackets mine. This statement was made
in the midst of discussion on spiritual gifts.)

"Therefore, you do not lack any spiritual gift as you eagerly wait
for our Lord Jesus Christ to be revealed."
(1 Corinthians 1:7)

I was in the early stages of teaching a Sunday School class that had all to do with the practical dynamics of spiritual gifts. As was my custom, we spent some time in a teaching mode and then spent the rest of our time in "clinic," in application, which was a time of learning to listen and hear Holy Spirit and then follow through with his communiques. Every week this portion of the class would start slow – and end with everyone wanting to stay for more! I had everyone simply be quiet for 120 seconds and wait to see what Holy Spirit might say. After that, I would ask who heard what. This particular week all was quiet initially. And then came, "All I heard was the word *toaster*." I remained quiet and let the class process. After a bit, a woman, who was a single mom with children and not much money, said with tears, "My toaster just broke this morning and it is an important tool in the lives of my children." To which another classmate said excitedly, "We were just talking about an extra toaster we have and what to do with it!" My son would say, "Boom!" This is spiritual gifts in action!

The word, "toaster" was a Word of Knowledge – a piece of knowledge known by God and not known by the recipient of the Word, for use by Holy Spirit in the life of another. Father knew of the broken toaster, and the need of the single mom. And he knew of the couple with an extra toaster. He brought the Word to a third person so as to connect the dots! All of this is from his heart of love and his care for people, even in the things that might seem trite to us. Go God! Action taken; gift received! Let's enter into the opportunity God is offering within the dynamics of spiritual gifts.

The New Testament is replete with references to, and examples of, spiritual gifts. There are twenty-nine different identifiable spiritual gifts within the New Testament. God has used the many people comprising the Kingdom and its Church, from Pentecost through today, in all nations, tribes, and tongues in the manifestations of spiritual gifts.

The beauty of these gifts is that they are not created or intended for their own purposes. They are tools of the Spirit used by the Spirit for the advancement of the Kingdom of God, used and exercised through the servants of the King. That is you and me, if we are willing.

Spiritual gifts are defined as, _a manifestation of Holy Spirit enabling one to minister, within a God-given spiritual dynamic, to the needs of others as the Spirit leads; it is a gift of grace._

For example, if Julia has a broken arm and Holy Spirit tells me to pray over her and ask for a healing, and she gets healed, who got the gift? We are talking about the spiritual gift of healing clearly identified in 1 Corinthians 12:9. These gifts are gifts of the Spirit; they belong to Holy Spirit. Who got the gift? Julia did. She is healed. Who am I in this equation? Nothing. A piece of conduit through whom the Spirit chose to flow. Was this transaction about the Spirit, Julia, the gift, or me? It was about God in his love and then about Julia, as she was the final recipient.

The gifts, created and offered by God, are not intended for him but for his use in ministering his love and compassion to his people. Genius, this Creator of ours. Brilliant in his ways, in his methodologies in pouring out his love for us. He thought and spoke the entire universe into existence. In our example, he could have healed Julia's arm with just a thought. But instead, he created things in such a way that includes his people, all of them that are willing.

**In his love and his sovereignty God chooses to minister to his people through his people.**

Quite brilliant. But also quite risky!

The gifts of the Spirit are simply the tools he uses to accomplish that which he put into motion in the first place. If you think about it, these gifts could be considered a commodity of his Kingdom. A commodity is defined as "an article of... commerce; especially a product as distinguished from a service. Something of use, advantage, or value." Synonyms include, "an asset, product, or property."[3]

The gifts of the Spirit are elements of Holy Spirit, and when used by him become manifestations of him. The word *gift* finds its root in the word *grace*. These gifts are grace-gifts; they have been referred to as "gracelets," because they are manifestations of the grace of God.[4] In the context of their expression, their materialization, they are used or used up. In that context, they could be seen as a product. They certainly are "of use, advantage, or value." The point is that if they are a commodity, they are without end. There is no need to replenish as the Spirit of God is ever present and ever willing to express and pour out his love and compassion. Again, these gifts are a type of tool for the job, Holy Spirit's tools to manifest the heart of the Father. In the example of Julia's broken arm, the motive and the purpose behind the healing is, over and over again, the desire of the Triune God to invest himself in the lives of his creation, from his heart to ours.

Consider this story:

> "A perplexed church member approached her pastor, 'How do I discover what God wants to do with my life? I feel that I'm drifting, I need direction. I want to live a good life, I want to do God's will, but how do I discover what that is for me?' Her question, grounded in a sincere faith commitment, has much in common with the struggle of the contemporary [twenty-first century] church to find purpose and relevance. But it also reflects the fundamental individualism, privatism, and self-preoccupation of modern [western] Christianity.
>
> The challenge for those involved in church transformation is to reformat the question from 'What should I [or we] be doing?' to '*What is God doing?*' As long as the emphasis is upon the human person, either individually or corporately, the

struggle will not be resolved. Persons of faith, and the church as the community of faith, are called to participate with God in accomplishing God's intent to bring all that exists *into the fulfillment of the Kingdom of God.* Only as we are able to discover and express God's overarching mission, a mission which transcends yet fulfills human desires and dreams, will authentic transformation occur within persons and church organizations."[5] (Emphasis and brackets mine)

"How do I discover what God wants to do with my life? How do I discover what that is for me?" That is a very sincere and powerful question, and one we have all asked, probably many times. And then the author nails it by answering the question with a question, "What is God doing?" In other words, if one will "Seek first his Kingdom and his righteousness..." (Matthew 6:33) they will discover exactly what God is doing -- and from that exactly what he wants to do with their life.

What God is doing is what God has always been doing: Pouring himself out on us in the context of us yielding to him, which in turn leads us to pour ourselves out on him. And in the same breath, we most easily come into this understanding in the context of spiritual gifts. This is why they exist. Back to the example of Julia's broken arm. He does not need us; he can do all things. But he likes us! He loves us, and wants to be with us and use us within his Kingdom. For his glory – and our gain.

The lady in the story above has a genuine concern. She is looking for purpose, for fulfillment in her life with God. Aren't we all looking for that? And for approval in the midst of that? Isn't that a major element in the human heart? And where are the answers found? Never within self. Never within society. Always within the tangible realities of one-on-one, deep, intimate relationship with Father God.

This is how he created it all. "As long as the emphasis is upon the human... the struggle will not be resolved."

I said at the beginning of this chapter that, "the beauty of these gifts is that they are not created or intended for their own purposes. They are tools of the Spirit used by the Spirit for the advancement of the Kingdom of God; *used and exercised through the servants of the King.* That is you and me, if we are willing." This is God's plan. This comprises his agenda for and with his creation, his kids. Again, that is you and me.

> ***The gifts of the Spirit, when understood and embraced, when eagerly desired, sought after, and received give direction, bring purpose, and cause fulfillment within our souls like nothing else on earth can.***

This is so powerful – and empowering.

Let's do a bit of a study in Romans 12:1-6 to open this up to see the Lord's heart even more:

> "¹Therefore, I urge you, brothers and sisters, in view of God's mercy, to offer your bodies as living sacrifices, holy and pleasing to God – this is your spiritual act of worship. ²Do not conform any longer to the pattern of this world, but be transformed by the renewing of your mind. Then you will be able to test and approve what God's will is (...that you may prove what the will of God is... NASB) – his good, pleasing, and perfect will. ³For by the grace given me I say to every one of you: Do not think of yourself more highly than you ought, but rather think of yourself with sober judgment, in accordance with the measure of faith God has

given you. ⁴Just as each of us has one body with many members, and these members do not all have the same function, ⁵so in Christ we who are many form one body, and each member belongs to all the others. ⁶We have different gifts, according to the grace given us." (Paul then goes on to list seven of the twenty-nine gifts.)

What are we doing when we offer ourselves as living sacrifices? We are yielding, we are "thinking of ourselves with sober judgment," we are submitting to him. What is the pattern of this world? Me, me, me. But what, or who, are you being transformed into? Jesus. Into his likeness, into the depth of relationship with God you were created for in the first place. What are we being formed into? Into one body belonging to him and to each other, again, for his glory and for our gain. It is a beautiful picture of Father's creation flowing and functioning as he first intended.

This is his plan. And this brings definition to his purpose for us all. This gives life to the practical and powerful statements found in Acts, Romans, and Revelation. Acts 7:28 says, "For in him we live and move and *have our being.*" Romans 4:17 refers to, "...the God who... *calls into being* things that were not." And Revelation 4:11 says, "...for you created all things, and *by your will* they were created and *have their being.*" (Emphasis mine) Does this not answer the questions the lady in the story – and all of us throughout the ages – have been crying out for forever? Is it not here that we fully *find* and truly *have* our *being*? I believe so.

Oh, by the way, the teaching that is out there that speaks to the three wills of God – the good and pleasing and perfect wills of God in verse two? Straight up, that is just *horrible* theology. God is. He is, "I Am" and "I Am as I Am" and "I Am the Great I Am." Period. There are no levels, no variants in the Sovereign God of the Universe. (John 8:58; Exodus,3:14; Ezekiel 38:23) That his will is good, pleasing, and perfect is not three different wills but one will being expressed in a triune manner.

Here is the list of the twenty-nine Spiritual Gifts, from Acts 16, Romans 12, Galatians 2, Ephesians 3 and 4, Colossians 4, 1 Corinthians 7, 12, and 13 and 1 Peter 4:

Prophecy	Administration
Serving	Hospitality
Teaching	Preaching
Exhortation	Missionary
Giving	Intercession
Leadership	Worship
Mercy	Word of Wisdom
Celibacy	Word of Knowledge
Voluntary Poverty	Discerning of Spirits
Martyrdom	Faith
Apostle (Delegate)	Healing
Prophet (Spokesman)	Miracles
Evangelist	Prophesy
Pastor (Shepherd)	Tongues
Teacher	Interpretation of Tongues
Helps	Exorcism

This list has thirty-two gifts listed. There is an overlap in words. There is prophecy, prophet, and prophesy; and then there is teaching and teacher. Eliminating the overlap brings the total to twenty-nine. There is an argument that suggests that the word worship is not actually listed as a gift and should not be included. The reality of worship is found throughout the Bible, Old and New Testaments. It is a strong expression of the connection between God and humanity. Thus, its inclusion. The three words in parentheses are alternative words. They are perhaps a more accurate translation from Greek to

English. Certainly, they are less conflictual, or in some cases, less fearful. I say the latter because in our culture the word pastor, in the context of being called, is often a fearful thing. This is a byproduct of a system run amuck.

Within the context of identifying and understanding spiritual gifts, it is valuable to understand what they are – and what they are not. Spiritual gifts are not talents, skills, or roles. They are a distinct capacity to minister supernaturally through the exclusive unction of Holy Spirit. Talents come in varying degrees and may seem to parallel a gift, but they are not the same. To be gifted in some particular task or area of life is a talent, not a spiritual gift. Spiritual gifts are not super-charged talents. Gifts are offered; they are not permanent. Talents are given; they are developed but they are always with you. A skill is an acquired ability. Spiritual gifts could be seen as acquired but only for the occasion for which they are intended. And a role is a responsibility, a required ability. It is "a prescribed pattern of behavior corresponding to an individual's status in a particular group."[6]

Spiritual gifts are not behavior patterns. They are also not for the having in that they are gifts of the Spirit – not gifts of humanity. They are not owned. It is Holy Spirit's decision as to who will flow with what gift and when that will happen. We cannot muster a gift, and to try to do so is quite contradictive to the heart and intent of God. It is important to understand that Holy Spirit can use anyone he chooses in the manifestations of his gifts at any time he wants. We don't earn them. (1 Corinthians 12:7; 1 Peter 4:10)

Don't be confused. It is obvious that many of the gifts describe activities that are common and even expected of followers of Jesus, yet there is a difference. For example, not all have the gift of hospitality but all are called to be hospitable. Not all have the gift of serving or evangelist, but all are called to serve and evangelize. Perhaps the best example is that of faith. We all have faith; it is a gift and also a fruit. (Ephesians 2:8-9 and Galatians 5:22 respectively) But the spiritual gift of faith is a supernatural phenomon of a much different dynamic that usually precedes another gift such as miracles, healing, or exorcism.

There is one more thing we should consider. Within the context of work assignments, when one is working in an area where they feel a "fit," it is going well for them. But if they have an assignment that is not a good fit, they get frustrated and feel incomplete. A similar thing can happen in the context of spiritual gifts. For example, Leadership, Administration, Pastor (Shepherd), Teacher, and Preacher are five different spiritual gifts. The classic problem is that within the Church system, it is assumed they are all one, and very few actually flow within that gift mix. It needs to be understood that in the Kingdom and its expressions, it is not so. When flowing within one's given gift mix there is fulfillment. When flowing outside of that there is at minimum frustration, and at maximum burn-out and hope deferred. And what do we have all over Christendom? Burn-out and hope deferred. Let's let God determine and lead, and not the assumptions within the system.

In the consideration of developing the natural flow of spiritual gifts within any Gathering, it is important to create an environment wherein they can flourish and prosper. One must build a sense of expectation within the group. If shepherd Johnny is focused on tithing, he will have a tithing people. If praying, then praying. If holiness, then holiness. You get the point. Let's be people that focus on God, and the things of his Kingdom, in such a way that the gifts become highly sought and highly demanded. Teach on them, focus on them, and learn to exercise them. They need to be stirred up. And how is that done? By keeping them on everyone's mind, and from there in their hearts. Pray into them. Look for them. Point them out when they show up. Encourage people. Doing this will lead to abundant manifestations of spiritual gifts in your midst, spilling over into the rest of your lives.

CHAPTER FIFTEEN

THE ESSENCE OF LEADING
A HOME GATHERING

**"Leadership is about developing and delegating
others to join in the work of Jesus."**[1]

W ithout criticism or critique, I can honestly say I have
learned more in the trenches of life and ministry than
I ever learned in the Masters and Doctorate degrees I
carry. This chapter reflects those trenches. It is aimed at sharpening
the concepts, principles, and skills of biblical leadership and the
raising up of leaders.

The most important thing to remember regarding leadership,
and the first matter of this chapter, whether you are a leader, or are
developing into one, is to *walk alongside*.

**Leadership is based on relationship and truly is an art form
that is much more caught than taught.**

So, learn to walk it out together.

I once was invited into an outside sales representative position
within a major national company. My "training" consisted of a brief
conversation with the regional manager wherein he pointed out my
territory on a wall map, talked briefly about polishing the apple, gave
me the keys to the van that was assigned to me, and sent me out the
door! Yeah, don't do that. *Walk alongside.*

"Build a people who will rise to your level of expectation in the Lord [to your level of faith and trust, enthuo and spiritual forcefulness (from Matthew 11:12)] instead of having a people who cause you to live at their level of existence."[2] (Brackets mine)

"A leader's failure to empower others is one of the key reasons some teams are ineffective [or some ministries fall short or fail]."[3] (Brackets mine)

Transformational leadership is accurately defined as doing with people what is best for them, and taking people where they need to go -- even if they don't like it or don't want to. This is not to force, push, or control. And this is certainly not to take them where you want them to go. It is to minister as Jesus did -- under the unction and leadership of Holy Spirit. If Sam is at point F and Holy Spirit is wanting to move him to point K, he will provide the grace and courage needed to make that move. Ours is not to push. Ours is to pray for that person and guide them as the Lord leads. Nothing more, nothing less. Consider how Jesus lead Peter in John 21:15-17:

> "...Jesus said to Simon Peter, 'Simon son of John, do you truly *love* me more than these?' 'Yes, Lord,' he said, 'you know that I *love* you.' Jesus said, 'Feed my lambs.' Again Jesus said, 'Simon son of John, do you truly *love* me?' He answered, 'Yes, Lord, you know that I *love* you.' Jesus said, 'Take care of my sheep.' The third time he said to him, 'Simon son of John, do you *love* me?' ...He said, 'Lord, you know all things; you know that I *love* you.'" (Emphasis mine)

On the surface, this passage seems redundant but fairly straight up. Jesus is engaging Peter for the purposes of reinstating him after he had denied Jesus three times. But there is so much more here. There are four Greek words that translate into English as *love*, two of which are used in this passage. One is *agape*, which basically means, "to [highly] esteem, to love indicating an [act] of the will."[4] The other is *phileo*, which means, "to love indicating feelings [and] warm affection."[5] The first interchange has Jesus asking Peter if he loves him using the Greek word *agape*, to which Peter says he loves him using the Greek word *phileo*. The second interchange is the same. But in the third interchange Jesus shifts to the word *phileo* when he asks him if he loves him, to which Peter says that he does *phileo* Jesus. Catch the difference, the shift? The difference is quite profound.

The point is the manner in which Jesus is handling Peter. He is challenging Peter with the word for love that is the deepest, that reflects the innermost commitment to another. Peter cannot respond in like manner. His broken heart cannot honestly return the statement back to Jesus on the same level, so he speaks to a friendship-type love. The same is the case with the second interchange. When Jesus asks the question the third time, he changes his approach by changing the word he uses. In that action he is adjusting and meeting Peter *just where he is*. This is huge as it clearly demonstrates the heart of Jesus in his willingness to meet Peter – and all of us – right where we are. He loves and embraces Peter in the midst of his brokenness. Powerful. This is an excellent example of how to lead.

It is important to remember that people will function at whatever level they are at when they join your group. If they come in with little or no vision or connected game plan, they will sit right there, even if later a vision and game plan are introduced. If they come in expecting encounters with God, they will stay engaged until and while those encounters are happening. You are the leader in this – so lead.

At the same time, within your own heart, "If you change your expectations it results in God actually changing what he will do [in you and through you]."[6] (Brackets mine)

I once spent time in a trade school learning, among many other things, how to sharpen drill bits. This might seem trite – until it is you that has to drill a hole through tempered steel! As one soon discovers, drill bit sharpening is an art form; it takes finesse and is not easy! The desired angle for a drill bit, for general use, is 118 degrees. If there is too much angle the bit will cut amazingly – and then quickly overheat and burn out. If there is too little an angle the bit is ineffective at actually cutting, and very little will be accomplished.

Can you see where this analogy is going? Leadership is like this. Be it one person or a team, if the expression of leadership is too strong – too much push or too much control – the point person will over-extend, overheat, and burn-out. And if there is too little actual leading, as in a lead-by-committee situation, it quickly becomes too shallow and there will be no progress. This analogy definitely does illuminate the Church today! The truth of it is that leading is also an art form and finding that correct "angle" is hard work.

Realize that God is moved by hearts, not by context.
He is moved by a willingness, not by a skill level.

You are ready right now for the assignment he is giving you.

Let's mature you on the journey.

The leader is in a continual state of training and growing with the understanding that at the point in life that we quit learning we quit growing and we begin stagnating. The Kingdom of God is quite fluid and dynamic in its nature, and thus is ever advancing. Consequently, if we are not proactively moving forward with it, we are by default going backward.

Fear is a major factor in this type of ministry because it is Spirit-led and not man-led. This means it is outside your control, which is most often a cause of fear in the first place. Truly, the only way around fear is through it. If one is not willing to take a risk by walking in faith, one will never work through the fear. Who is the author of faith? Jesus. What is the opposite of fear? Love. "There is no fear in love, but perfect love casts out fear." And Jesus is that perfect love. (1 John 4:18) Understand this, and ask the Lord to help you learn to work through it.

Instead of controlling, work at equipping and training people, and releasing them into the ministry to which they are called. Be willing to take a risk and allow mess. Throw out professionalism. Focus on the journey – and never on the destination. You are a family, hopefully growing and working together toward healthiness. Embrace the mess! Ever raise a family? This is the same thing.

> **If you cannot allow and embrace the**
> **messiness then it is still about you**
> **and you are not leading as you ought.**

Bring people in with a high level of determination to make this thing all that it can be – and in Christ it will get there! Bring people in with an open door to Jesus as the center and reason for it all - and by the unction and anointing of Holy Spirit it will get there! Cast vision repeatedly. Help people, especially leaders and potential leaders, capture the reality of the vision. Start a fire and get some enthusiasm going. Enthuo, enthuo, enthuo.

In the movie *Gandhi*, he was quoted saying, "There go my people and I must follow them, for I am their leader."[7] That statement is quite the paradox. And yet it is very accurate and illuminous of today's circumstances, and fairly well illustrates the quandary of the Church. I continue to find it amazing how little most leaders really know and understand about themselves and their calling, its value and importance, and from that about the Father's heart for his people. Ouch. I believe that if we could all come to the deep truth about exactly who we are in Christ, most of the struggles and hardships of ministry, most of the difficulties with direction and purpose, would evaporate away. I think the enemy believes that as well and that is why he spends so much time working at beating us up with one lie after another. (John 8:44c, 10:10a) Let's work to capture this fully.

As leaders, especially at this point in history, *we are to be quite active in the equipping process*. In this, we need to be aware of the system. The system that puts leaders into a place and a mindset wherein they are forced to spend the majority of their time and energy *reacting* instead of *acting*. They spend their time putting out fires and responding to those who petition or solicit them. This is all well and good - and necessary. But it is the good that is not the best.

I do not see Jesus or Paul *reacting* nearly as much as I see them *acting*, as in taking action.

Reacting is more passive. Acting is more of an intentional pursuit. There is a huge difference between the two. One brings acceptance while the other demonstrates approval. One offers acknowledgment while the other delivers encouragement and exhortation - and thus motivation. One breeds little or no growth, while the other stirs and energizes people on to maximum potential in Christ. I believe one is more the heart of man while the other is more the heart of the Father.

Give consideration to the Starbucks model of doing business. Much of what they do can be adjusted and worked into a leadership model, especially within the context of Gatherings. There is an unseen intentionality to be found within their system. On the front side of the bar, they have created an atmosphere that is casual and comfortable where you and your friends can enjoy the surroundings, the coffee, and each other. On the backside of the bar there is a well-oiled machine that is anything but casual. They have a system that works well at bringing you what you want. They are simply humming along while you enjoy the ambiance, at your pace and comfort level. They put in the work so you don't have to.

Bringing that example into the Home Gathering setting, if you as a leader do the work, come prepared in heart and mind, in spirit and in intellect, offering a warm and relaxed atmosphere, people will respond in like manner. And your times together will flow harmoniously, effectively, and productively. Creating this environment, this arena if you will, lends itself excellently to the seamless flowing of the Four Elements we previously discussed.

Said another way, if you bring the tension of anxiety, uncertainty, and insecurity from within your own soul, you will propagate the same within the souls of others. Or if you bring an arrogance or haughtiness to the group, you will produce the same – or a negative response -- in your followers. We reproduce what we model, for better or worse. Relax. Let God be God. It is his gig; let him have his way in it. Do the work required of you with intention and diligence. Do it well and in advance of your Gathering. And then settle into Holy Spirit and follow his lead. Ephesians 4:1b-3 says, "...live a life worthy of the calling you have received. Be completely humble and gentle; be patient, bearing with one another in love. Make every effort to keep the unity of the Spirit [and unity with the Spirit] through the bond of peace." (Brackets mine)

Within this model of ministry, the leadership structure is designed to be mostly flat in appearance and function. It is not, and it can never be, about a man, about a person. It must always be about Holy Spirit being the leader. This results in more people doing things that are relevant in the Kingdom, more people finding fulfillment in their lives through Kingdom activity, less people getting burned-out, and no people getting the attention or the glory.

Perhaps one of the best sections of New Testament Scripture to consider regarding leadership is Ephesians 4:1b-16. Let's look at verses 11-16 as well as 4:8b, which states that, "he... gave gifts to men." The context of these passages has to do with unity in the body of Christ. Within this unity are points of identification regarding leaders and then directives for leaders. Leaders either bring unity or division; you choose.

"[11]It was he who gave some to be apostles, some to be prophets, some to be evangelists, and some to be pastors and teachers, [12]to prepare God's people for works of service, so that the body of Christ may be built up [13]until we all reach unity in the faith and in the knowledge of the Son of God and become mature, attaining to the whole measure of the fullness of Christ. [14]Then we will no longer be infants, tossed back and forth by the waves, and blown here and there by every wind of teaching... [15]Instead, speaking the truth in love, we will in all things grow up into him who is the Head, that is, Christ. [16]From him the whole body... grows and builds itself up in love as each part does its work."

Down through time, there are entire volumes that have been offered on this section of Scripture, some of them quite excellent, some not so much. It is not my intent to reinvent the wheel but to simply point out some of the core insights for our perusal.

First, it needs to be seen that within this entire section there is one primary noun and one primary verb. They are used twice for emphasis, once in verse 8 and again in verse 11. They are *he* and *gave*. He gave. The he is the Christ. Jesus gave. The entire communication is built around him and his actions. The original writing translated says it this way, "He himself indeed gave..." The word *indeed* brings a double emphasis to the giving, which in turn brings that same emphasis back to the *he*. That is why it translates with "He himself," and with "indeed gave."

There are many teachings on this out there. Unfortunately, some of them are quite erroneous. The emphasis is on, and must stay on, who is doing what. Yes, the Lord is working through people, but it is never about them. This is supported and confirmed in the closing statement of the section, verse 16, when it says, "From him..." He gave; all that is given is from him.

He gave. For what purpose? To prepare, to equip, the saints. Again, for what purpose? For the works of service. Why? For the building up of the body of Christ. Who is doing the building? Under his direction, the saints, which comprise the body.

Let's take this a bit further. The word *prepare* in verse 12 is the word *equip* in the KJV and literally means "to set the bone."[8] It is to put back in place that which has been broken. That which is broken is the saint. Also, the word *saint* means "set apart," "the set apart ones."[9] It refers to anyone who has said yes to Jesus and is born again, and has nothing to do with the doctrine of sainthood found within a particular part of Christendom. And he is doing this why? Again, for the works of service. For work, for ministry in his Kingdom, to those within his Kingdom. And this so that the body may be built up. This is edification and encouragement, spiritual growth and advancement.

This is why we are here! This sets the table for our place and purpose within him. This is so powerful; it gives us value and reason for being. Stop. Think. Receive. I'll say it again, it gives us value and our reason for our being here on this planet. Wow.

All this speaks "to his Kingdom economy, which is his divine plan for humanity from beginning to end."[10] And as a leader, you are given opportunities to aid and assist in the facilitation of it all. Pretty heady stuff. Might be best to take it seriously, and let Holy Spirit do his work in training you for it.

By the way, to *set the bone* applies itself, in part, to addressing head-on the challenges, the weaknesses, and the struggles we all have in our humanity as we work to live out this life. To set the bone is often just as painful as breaking the bone. But how else will it heal and be strong, true, and useful again? This says to me that the art of leading, of shepherding, is comforting, consoling, and encouraging. It is also exhorting, confronting, and challenging when need be. It is truth in love. It is love in truth.

Also to be considered is that the spiritual gift of leadership is often latent. It needs to be birthed. Most often those with the gift will not lead – unless they see a void or a need, and then they will step in. Create that positive void for them. Give it birth.

We must realize and remember that we are not counselors, fix-it agents, or the answer men and women. We are caregivers, listeners, encouragers, exhorters, and pray-ers.

What follows are a series of strategies from the trenches that will help you grow as a leader and/or fine tune your existing leadership skills.

- Learn to flow in what I call the Ministry of Presence. Come alongside in work and play, in rejoicing and grieving. When there is need, lend a hand. Be proactive in leading by example and by speaking into people's lives as the Lord leads. Do this as a brother or sister through transformational leadership. Most of all, just be there. Often people are not looking for an answer, they simply need a friend, a listening heart. Be that person.

- Please recognize the call to ownership. The more you involve people, the more you include them and delegate to them, the more they grow in ownership. "This is my Gathering," or better yet, "This is our Gathering," is a great thing to hear. In this context, as you and your followers continue to grow and develop, it is fair to say that the Gathering will go as far as you take it.

- Be diligent in developing commitment. Your level of commitment will, in direct proportion, determine your effectiveness and success as a leader. Your investment is paramount. Leaders lead by investing themselves in the lives of those placed under and around them. Said again, your Gathering will go as far as you take it.

The Lord is willing and able to make you willing and able.

- Points of Challenge with Solutions:

DR. JAY SLIFE

- How to stir up, challenge, and encourage people so as to build leaders? Model a style of leadership that is energetic, encouraging, and attractive; they will follow your lead.
- How to establish a stronger, more active, more fluid line of communication amongst leaders and upcoming leaders? Again, model a style of leadership that is clearly and specifically communicative. Engage and invest in others and they will learn to follow suit. Communicate clearly and completely, assuming and hiding nothing. Be genuinely humble, always and forever. Become an excellent pursuer! Become an excellent listener!
- What to do about the issue of trusting leaders? Create and maintain an arena of trust by demonstrating it with intentionality. We must pray, delegate, monitor, mentor, and release. Always remember it can be messy. Understand that mistakes will be made by all; it is how we learn. Learn to laugh, absorb, and go forward positively together. If you can laugh at yourself others will learn to do the same regarding themselves. Life is so much more enjoyable when we can learn to lighten up! It is only drama if you make it drama.
- How do you *actively* delegate? Just do it! Just let go! Again, it is about being willing to take a risk. Pray and delegate. As delegation is extended, so are responsibilities and accountabilities. In this, trust will build and fruit will grow! People are smarter and more willing than one might give them credit for. Learn to lean on Holy Spirit, and in that, let him teach you how to trust others. The key is to include accountability checks within the relationship. This brings encouragement to the ones learning, and peace to you! Bring them honest questions from the heart that require honest answers. The more honest and vulnerable you are, the more they will

be. Create a feedback system, which includes regular personal contact with each leader. Give them *permission* to engage and invest in others and watch them rise to the occasion.

An age-old question is are leaders born or built?
The true answer is yes!

The biggest challenge comes in bringing the intangible elements of quality leadership into the tangible and giving it away to those who are called to walk in it. This involves finding and developing motivated, driven, dedicated, determined, and righteous men and women willing to invest, sacrifice, and actually rise to the challenge of leading.

The biggest question is how do I identify, raise up, and release such creatures? There must be a desire within them and it is on you and Holy Spirit to create one. It must be about a team and never about an individual, especially you. Then it must be about proactive leadership, which means taking initiative and not being afraid to lead and *becoming* a leader, a shepherd. This means stepping into the call and all it entails, bringing large doses of encouragement, and being courageous enough to give people permission to simply be themselves. And always resisting the temptation to turn it into a system, a program.

Leadership truly is an art form! It is like dancing, but never a solo performance. It requires being fluid and sensitive to the place and the placement of others. It is setting the other up for success, in God's way. It is always about the other, first him and then others. It is Fred Astaire and Grace Kelly who were two of the best dancers ever. They were continually interacting, continually re-engaging and re-discovering. Here re-engaging equals re-discovering, which equals fun, joy, excitement, affirmation, being together, feeling included, and approved of.

All of these are essential human needs.

There must be eye contact, not too much, not too little. It needs to be natural and comfortable. Come to realize that if you ask the right question you can be quiet for 20 minutes! Come prepared and relaxed. Come sensitized by and to Holy Spirit. I keep saying this, but it is so essential: You are leading, so lead. They are following, they will do and be what and who you are! Be engaged, passionate, compassionate, and fun. Flow in enthuo. Learn to excel in interactive teaching. Never interrupt. Never allow interruption. Resist the temptation to preach! Resist the temptation to be at the center, to be the focus. Way too many leaders are where they are, have worked their way to where they are, in a negative way because they continue to be impressed with their own voice. Do not be that person!

The Lord delights in the way of the man
whose steps he has made firm;
though he stumble, he will not fall, for the
Lord upholds him with his hand.
(Psalms 37:23-24)

CHAPTER SIXTEEN

ON VOCATIONAL LEADERSHIP

"I had succumbed to the all-too-prevalent work hierarchy that considers full-time employment in the Church more spiritual [which assumes more important] than secular vocations."[1] (Brackets mine)

This statement captures well first, the arrogance found within much of professional Christendom, and second, the deeply engrained understanding that the only way of ministry is paid ministry. "This world view did long ago create a life, a perception, of its own. Perceptions can do that. A long time ago, as in back to Constantine and the melding of the Church into the then-current socio-political-economic system commonly and generally referred to as government, the Church became systematized and sunk into a predominantly man-made entity. The Protestant Reformation did much. It did not change this issue as the Church was still not fully focused upon lordship. And this now to the place where much or even most of today's Church is patterned entirely after a secular corporate model of doing business. Some have called it CEO Christianity. Not that there is anything inherently wrong with the corporate business model so common amongst us. But for the most part it is distinctly not a biblical model."[2]

I would be remiss if I didn't address the understandings and expectations surrounding vocational leadership. It is my belief, based on what is clear from the New Testament, that the preferred model of ministry is what has been called *lay-based ministry*. "Yes, the terminology of *lay* and *clergy*, or *professional*, are over-used within the Church and under-supported from the Scripture. And this since the Third Century, which is the 200's."[3] (Emphasis mine)

Lay comes from *laity*, as in the opposite of *clergy*. *Clergy* has always been seen within the understanding of paid, professional people. *Lay* then, within the confines of the Church, has always been understood as non-professional or perhaps voluntary.

"Throughout much of Christian history, followers of Christ have been classified as either lay or clergy. In practice, lay is contrasted with clergy, or cleric. 'Cleric,' with the fact of 'ordination,' is based on the later influence of the Latin term 'ordo.' [We obtain the English word 'order' from this word.] Because of the common perception that lay is a lesser state than cleric, on the basis of the lack of ordination, the term lay has the connotation of lacking skills, knowledge, and preparation …this from the 3rd Century. [This was further] obscured by [the development of] monasticism. Thus, the laity [was] seen in contrast to the clergy on the level of leadership and activity, and… in contrast to the monk on the level of holiness [and spirituality]."[4] (Brackets mine)

Of course, this is not true. It is simply an order created by man for the purposes of controlling the masses. Corruption runs deep in the heart of humanity. The perception, then and now unfortunately, is that one is not qualified to minister unless they have some kind of education and/or some kind of credentials and/or some kind of ordination. This perception has been wrong since its inception. In its original context, laity was actually a demeaning term, not unlike how the Sadducees and Pharisees thought of and handled the common man in their day. Is it any different today?

This is one of the main reasons why there is such a struggle within the principles and perceptions of leadership in the Church at large today. None of the above is found or established from the Bible. Within the Church at large, the principles and directives of leadership are almost totally built on the traditions of man, and clearly not on the teachings of Scripture. But the truth can set us free! (John 8:32)

If we are born-again, we are part of a royal priesthood. (1 Peter 2:9) And we are called to full-time ministry. (Ephesians 4:12, 16) The truth is that there is no real support for professional ministry to be found in the New Testament, and there is certainly no support for any professional ministry as an exclusive right for the few.

The point here is simply this: Leaders do their best by gaining their financial support primarily from what is commonly referred to as tent-making. (Acts 18:3) This is the New Testament model found repeatedly in the lives of numerous New Testament characters, Jesus, Paul, Peter, and Luke to name just a few. We could refer to this as bi-vocational ministry in that most of the personal revenue comes from outside the realm of ministry. This is actually very freeing if you think about it since there is no pressure to perform, impress, or manipulate. There will no doubt be exceptions to this over time for a few. If the Home Gatherings grow into a network or networks there may be need to hire administrative personnel, because time will not permit them to be outside-vocational or bi-vocational.

**The model is to be one of sacrificial living
with a tent-making type vocation
establishing the financial base for the leader's life.
The New Testament is still our example.**

We should consider the use of the term *avocation*. And also the use of the word *hobby*.

Avocation is defined as, "something a person does in addition to a principal occupation, especially for pleasure," and, "a minor occupation undertaken as a diversion." The origins of the word suggest, "a calling away," which is away from a primary occupational endeavor and also from the routine of vocation. A synonym is "hobby."[5]

In the investment of time and energy toward the developing and leading of a Home Gathering, the ministry time could be seen as *hobby time*. The word hobby means "something a person likes to do or study in his/her spare time; favorite pastime or avocation [i.e., non-professional, non-paying]."[6] Another source says, "an activity or interest [intently] pursued for pleasure …and not as a main occupation."[7] (Brackets mine)

As an example, consider that there are 168 hours in a week. Let's do the math. Subtract 56 hours for sleep (7 days times 8 hours per day), 50 hours for work (5 days times 10 hours per day, which includes commute time), 20 hours for evenings at home (5 days times 4 hours per day), 21 hours for chores, errands, etc. (7 days times 3 hours per day), 3 hours for personal devotional time with your Lord (6 days times 30 minutes per day), and 3 hours for a corporate church encounter, should you so choose (1 day times 3 hours per day). Liberally, that adds up to 153 hours per week. Conservatively, that leaves you with 15 hours per week to invest in the *hobby* of ministry. That is investing in others, through Jesus, in ministry. That's a lot of time. Think about it.

When one considers these thoughts, and couples it with the grace, provisions, and protections of God within our lives, it becomes easy to understand that the biblical principle of avocational ministry is on the table for any and all to encounter and live within. Please give serious consideration to the invitation. Let's go there. Let's invite Holy Spirit to train us in living there.

If you are being stirred or convicted by Holy Spirit in the context of the chapters on leadership and avocational ministry, please be sure to read chapter seventeen, which addresses the shift away from professional ministry. Can you make the shift? The truth is that with the Lord's help, yes, you can. It comes down to who – or what - is lord of your life, and what exactly is your calling.

CHAPTER SEVENTEEN

TO THOSE STARTING AGAIN OR BEING SHIFTED BY GOD

This is for those considering – or being pushed into - a shift in your style of ministry. Or for those potentially moving out of the expression of one calling and into another. This is for those who are being convicted by Holy Spirit to allow him to broaden or expand their heart and understanding regarding a model or philosophy of ministry. For the many who have been so steeped in their tradition of ministry for so long yet find themselves now being stretched to consider, or re-consider, the realm of small group ministry as the mainstay of the ministry of our King in 2024 and beyond.

First and foremost, listen for -- and to -- the Lord. Resist the temptation to listen to self. Resist the temptation to listen to certain others that perhaps have their agenda in mind – and not the Lord's. Resist the temptation to listen to any others *until you have heard from God*. He is your Lord. He is the one that called you in the first place. He is the one who knows what is best. He is the one you need to be following. Yes, "There is wisdom in many counselors," (Proverbs 11:22) but there is also a time when only God can rightfully speak and direct your path. Wait to hear from God, and make no move until you do. Do not allow it to be about you, your pride and fears. Only allow it to be about his love and adoration toward you and those you are to shepherd.

Beware of the good that is not the best.
Your Lord has your best in mind.

Beware of bitterness and all its trappings, most of which are unforgiveness and forms of deception. Many a decision has been made; many a resultant pain has been experienced within the ensnarement of bitterness in the soul. Do not make decisions by way of vengeance, of the I'll-show-you heart and mentality. Instead, let go of the pride and the fear and let your Lord help you learn from your mistakes and shortcomings.

Realize that change is difficult and does not come easy. Especially with age. It seems that the older we get the more afraid we become. Things are moving too fast. Change is all around us. There is the unknowing of it, the uncertainty of it. And yet, it seems that often it is within the latter years, perhaps the latter third of life, that our Lord brings us to shift, to change. And at least potentially to the fullness of our calling. It is *within the change* that his best shines forth. Will we agree with him? Will we cooperate with his workings in our hearts? Will we yield and say yes to him? Or will we become and/or stay frozen in our own little world?

Again, do not allow the pain, the hurt, the embarrassment, the pride, or the independent spirit to rule. This is the time in your life where the sweetness of humility and a yielded heart can rise up more than ever before. This is that time where the peace of God that surpasses all understanding can protect you and keep you closer than you have ever been to Jesus and Father God. You choose; your choice. (Please consider reading the author's book, *First Things First Revised Edition*, a significant breakdown of the Beatitudes that speaks fully into the work of Holy Spirit regarding, among other things, lordship in your life.)

In Joshua chapter one, Yahweh said to Joshua, "Be strong and courageous" three times! In the midst of this communique, he also says, "...you will lead" "Obey... do not turn to the right or to the left..." "...be successful wherever you go..." "Meditate on [me] day and night..." "Do not be afraid; do not be discouraged, for the

Lord your God will be with you wherever you go." (Joshua 1:6-9, brackets mine)

It is critical to see here that Father God is not calling Joshua out because he is weak and cowardly, which is the opposite of strong and courageous. What Father is doing is reminding Joshua of who he is, of what he has already developed within him. Joshua is eighty years old at this time in his life. He has walked with God all those years. Father has built him to this place. He is now bringing encouragement and exhortation to Joshua's heart from that building. And to yours, if you will let him.

The statement, "Where God guides, God provides" is a reasonable application of Isaiah 58:11. It says, "The Lord will guide you always; he will satisfy your needs in a sun-scorched land and will strengthen your frame. You will be like a well-watered garden, like a spring whose waters never fail." (You do well to read, study, and meditate on the entirety of Isaiah 58. Father has much to say to you from there.)

Consider the story of Gideon and his three-hundred warriors. (Judges 7) It is a story that speaks much. Its primary message has all to do with a confidence. A confidence that reflects God in the heart. What is the difference between the 300 men and the 9,700 men, or the twenty-two thousand men? An awareness outside of themselves. From which comes a confidence. But now as then, in our case, it is not self-confidence. No, it is a confidence in Jesus, a Christ-centered confidence.

With Gideon, the advance, the victory, was not based on self's ability. It was based on the confidence, the faith, the trust those men had in their God to do what he said he would do. They trusted! They trusted Gideon and they trusted their God. And the fears, the uncertainties, the doubts became not. Are you part of Gideon's 300? Are you a man or woman with that kind of faith and trust in God? If not, why not? It really is a tangible option. It is not something we create or build; that easily becomes a performance thing. It is a reception of, not a building of. Huge difference. The faith, the trust I need to walk at this level of confidence with my Lord does not come from me. It is, however, fully received by me within the practices of relationship and asking. As has been stated, my choice, your choice.

God will meet you where you decide to land.

I am including two brief writings that are apropos to what we've been discussing, and will provide more opportunity for Holy Spirit to work in your heart.

The High Calling

If God has called you to be really like Jesus in all your spirit, he will draw you into a life of crucifixion and humility, and put on you such demands of obedience, that he will not allow you to follow other Christians, and in many ways, he will seem to let other good people do things which he will not let you do.

Other Christians who seem very religious and useful may push themselves, pull strings, and work schemes to carry out their plans, but you cannot do it. And if you attempt it, you will meet with such failure and rebuke from the Lord as to make you sorely penitent.

Others can brag on themselves, their work, their success, their writings, but Holy Spirit will not allow you to do any such thing. And if you begin it, he will lead you into some deep mortification that will make you despise yourself and all your good works.

Others will be allowed to succeed in making great sums of money, or having an inheritance left to them, or in having luxuries. But God may supply you daily, because he wants you to have something far better than gold. And that is a helpless dependence on him, that he may have the privilege of providing your needs day by day out of his unseen treasury.

The Lord may let others be honored, and advanced, and keep you hid away in obscurity, because he wants to produce some choice, fragrant fruit for his coming glory, which can only be produced in the shade.

God will let others be great, but keep you small. He will let others do a work for him, and get the credit for it, but he will make you work and toil on without knowing how much you are doing. And then to make your work still more precious, he will let others get the credit for the work which you have done. And this will make your reward ten times greater when Jesus comes. Holy Spirit will put a strict watch on you with a jealous love, and will rebuke you for little words and feelings or for wasting your time, which other Christians never seem distressed over.

So, make up your mind that God is an infinite Sovereign. And has a right to do as he pleases with his own. He will not explain to you a thousand things, which may puzzle your reason in his dealings with you. God will take you at your word. And if you absolutely sell yourself to be his bond-servant, his slave, he will wrap you up in a jealous love, and let other people say and do many things that you cannot. Settle it forever, that you are to deal directly with Holy Spirit, and that he is to have the privilege of tying your tongue, or chaining your hand, or closing your eyes, in ways that others may never experience.

Now when you are so possessed with the living God that you are, in your secret heart, pleased and delighted over this peculiar, personal, private, jealous guardianship and management of Holy Spirit over your life, you will have found the entrance of heaven.[1]

Dying to Self

When you are forgotten, or neglected, or purposely set at naught, and you don't sting and hurt with the insult of the oversight, but your heart is joyful, being counted worthy to suffer for Christ, that is dying to self.

When your good is evil spoken of, when your wishes are crossed, your advice disregarded, your opinions ridiculed, and you refuse to let anger or hurt rise in your heart, or even defend yourself, but take it all in patient loving silence, that is dying to self.

When you lovingly and patiently bear any disorder, any irregularity, any impunctuality, or any annoyance; when you can stand face to face with waste, folly, extravagance, spiritual insensibility – and endure it as Jesus did, that is dying to self.

When you are content with any food, any offering, any raiment, any climate, any society, any solitude, any interruption by the will of God, that is dying to self.

When you never care to refer to yourself in conversation, or to record your own good works, or itch after commendation; when you can truly love to be unknown, that is dying to self.

When you can see your brother prosper and have his needs met, and can honestly rejoice with him in spirit and feel no envy, nor question God, while your own needs are far greater and in desperate circumstances, that is dying to self.

When you can receive correction and reproof from one of less stature than yourself, and can humbly submit inwardly as well as outwardly, finding no rebellion or resentment rising up within your heart, that is dying to self.

Are you dead yet?[2]

The truth is that the more you die the more you live. The more you die to self, the more you yield to the Lord's work in getting you past you, the more you live in him. That to which he is calling you requires of you your self, your life as you have built and maintained it. This is death. Ah, but this is life as he ordained it. And this death/life equation is the very thing required of you as you transition into the new life he has for you.

CHAPTER EIGHTEEN

ESSENTIAL PRINCIPLES

In this chapter, I have captured a number of principles that when followed enhance the life of any Gathering as it goes and grows in Jesus and his Kingdom dynamics. They are all learned from years of hands-on ministry, and truthfully many of them out of mistakes made! As the chapter title says, they are essential. Please be encouraged by them, and please learn from my errors and oversights!

1. Intercession: Pray it in

This is at the top of this list for good reason. The success of any Home Gathering is all about prayer. All. It has always been God's Kingdom, God's ministry to those within his Kingdom. He is King and that makes us not. We are subject to him, so we are subjects. We must learn to follow his lead. That starts with prayer, with interceding for the people, for the strategies and directives, for the directions and course corrections. Someone said it well when they said that many a ministry has failed or fallen short simply because they did not devote themselves to a lifestyle of prayer.

"History may be shaped in the halls of academia and powered by... politicians, but in the halls of heaven, history is shaped by intercessors. Do not live history. Dare to shape it. Revival precedes arrival. Prayer precedes revival. We have come to this threshold."[1]

Jesus only did what he saw his Father doing; by himself he could do nothing. (John 5:19,30. Paraphrase mine) This was his choice, an act of his will. He understood submission. He understood obedience.

His decision to follow Father was behind the whats, hows, and whys of his ministry. His prayer life was behind the decision. Many a time he, "went up on a mountain" to spend time with Father. It was in those times he gained the strength, the fortitude, and the internal ability to face and confront the wiles of the enemy and the harassment of humanity. His strength was not his own. Nor his wisdom or revelation. It all came to him by way of his prayer life.

Prayer is both an obligation and a privilege. It is also a gift. It is an acquired taste in that it is a discipline that needs to be developed. It is all too easy to forgo and forget. But the one who sees its value and has invited Jesus, the Chief Intercessor, to aid and assist in its development will know of its overwhelming power and significance. I started the second half of this book with this statement and these two Scriptures which are absolutely critical:

Psalm 127:1 Unless the Lord builds the house, its builders labor in vain.

1 Peter 2:5 You, like living stones, are being built into a spiritual house.

The only way we can get inside the will of the Creator, the only way we will see the house built, is within a lifestyle of prayer and intercession. Become an intercessor. Intercede for others. Ask others to intercede for you and yours. Develop the value of, and an arena of, intercession. You will not regret it.

People with any of these spiritual gifts fit well into this ministry: intercession, prophecy, discerning of spirits, tongues, interpretation of tongues, faith, serving, or leadership.

2. Holy Spirit

When Jesus ascended, he sent Holy Spirit to be our Helper. Without him we will not be able to live by his ways or fulfill our calling to him. If you are born-again, then your spirit becomes alive and coexists with Holy Spirit within you. This gives you the full opportunity to be Spirit-filled and Spirit-led. This is the only way to the fullness he died for and has offered to us.

John 10:10b says, "I have come that they [you] may have life, and have it to the full." The NASB says, "...and have it abundantly." (Brackets mine) Jesus accomplished this with his death, resurrection, and ascension. Holy Spirit is here to walk this out with us.

He is the Counselor, the one who comes alongside. (John 14:16) He is your Advocate working in support and defense of you. (John 16:7) He is the Teacher who will be ever present. (John 16:8) He is the Convicter of sins, for your growth and benefit, for the transformation of your life. (John 16:10) He is the Spirit of truth, guiding you into all truth and away from all lies and deceptions. (John 16:13) He is the Power Giver, the one who gives us the power we need to live it all out in and for him. (Acts 1:8) This power from on high is our only hope to accomplish the purposes of God, to advance his Kingdom; without it we are unable to fulfill the call. Said another way, we need the power of God to advance his Kingdom in the manner in which he intends.

Whether being "baptized in the Spirit" is something accomplished at the point of being born-again, or is a separate, second encounter is not something we will discuss here. Suffice it to say, again, if you are born-again then the Spirit of God, the Holy Spirit dwells within you. It is clear from Scripture that this is not a one-time event; it is actually intended to be an ongoing, over-the-course-of-life encounter. There are many infillings, many points of encounter with Holy Spirit. It is something that is a gift and not earned. It requires your willingness to receive from and yield to him.

This filling, or infilling, provides the power needed to do the works of his Kingdom.

The realm of his Kingdom, the realm of ministry defined, built, and maintained by him, the realm of an abundant life, all require his presence and his power. Holy Spirit is the Agent for all of that. The Fruits of the Spirit (Galatians 5:22-23), the Gifts of the Spirit (primarily in 1 Corinthians 12:4-11, but there are twenty-nine of them scattered around the New Testament), and what I call the Fruits of the Kingdom, are all from him and fully available to us through him. This is where he wants us to live!

It is imperative that this pursuit, this adventure, be of and by Holy Spirit. That is to say it must be Spirit-led, Spirit-directed, and especially Spirit-filled. Signs and wonders, power encounters, healings, deliverances, deep and significant heart changes authored and procured by the Spirit, worship, and prayer and intercession are all essential and come as a result of a delightful and fulfilling relationship with the Lord, of which Holy Spirit is a part.

3. Ministry is Intended to be Fun; Keep it Small, Keep it Simple

Jesus said in Matthew 11:29-30 "Take my yoke upon you and learn from me, for I am gentle and humble in heart, and you will find rest for your souls. For my yoke is easy and my burden is light." In this context, *easy* might be better translated as "fitting" or "fitted." Each yoke was custom made and fitted to the neck and shoulders of the ox so that heavy loads would not harm the animal. This is the intent of Jesus in what he said. He does not want you hurt or harmed. He does not want you to have to overlabor or overstress in life or ministry. The instruction to take his yoke upon you is him saying he is carrying the load. Learn to work, to walk, with him so as to find rest for your soul.

When built according to the Master, there is fun and fulfillment in ministry. Yes, there will be challenge, but the majority of it is not intended to be so. If your yoke doesn't fit it is time to reassess. Are you leading according to your own personality and nature, or are you trying to copy or mimic someone? Is your life balanced, or are you overworking in order to fulfill your understanding of ministry? Are you trying to live up to your own unreasonable expectations, or someone else's? Is what you are doing a good fit for you, or are you over extended into something that the Lord did not intend for you in the first place?

These are all great questions that need real and honest answers. The ministry God has for you is intended to flow from Holy Spirit through you, through your God-given personality, perspectives, and nature. He is not asking you to perform for him. Can you simply be you? Can you honor and respect yourself and your ways? Can you allow Holy Spirit to bring you to that place wherein you are flowing in a God-ordained confidence, a Christ-centered confidence within you?

Please realize that some struggles are brought for refining, wisdom, and to build trust in him. And other struggles come because of sin issues that he wants removed. Ask Holy Spirit to help you discern the difference, and then work with him to learn and grow. Let God deal with your fears and insecurities. If you think you don't have them you are fooling yourself. We all have them. It is why Jesus came in the first place. 2 Peter 1:5-8 says, "Make every effort to add to your faith goodness; and to goodness, knowledge; and to knowledge, self-control; and to self-control, perseverance; and to perseverance, godliness; and to godliness, brotherly kindness; and to brotherly kindness, love. For if you possess these qualities in increasing measure, they will keep you from being ineffective and unproductive in your knowledge of our Lord Jesus Christ, [and from there in the realm of ministry]." (Brackets mine) Realize his work is a process; the passage says, "in increasing measure."

Ministry is intended to be relational. From that statement, let Holy Spirit teach you how to relax and flow with it. Lead the way, don't control it. Genuinely invite, don't push or force. Don't try to fix things, that is not your job. Don't feel obligated to carry the load of the group, that is still not your job. Honor and respect others and you will be honored and respected. "Let your kindness be evident to all. The Lord is near." (Philippians 4:5)

Considering the principle of keeping it simple and small, the best ministry happens in small groups. Resist the temptation to build something. Most pastors in most churches are stressing to build bigger than the anointing they have been given to operate under. Don't do that. Stay small. If it grows, and it will, learn to delegate and to multiply it out. Learn to raise up leaders. Learn to give away; let the best people move on into their calling. It is not yours anyway. Small is more simple than large. Learn to be content there.

Catch this, the number of relational points or signals between two people is two. With three people it is nine. With five people it becomes seventy-five. By the time it becomes eight people the number jumps to one-thousand-sixteen. And when it reaches ten people there are over five-thousand different signals drifting around the room! No wonder Charlie and Jill can't make friends on Sunday morning in the local church. By keeping it small there are way more positive relational opportunities without becoming overwhelmed. Jesus took on a dozen men. That is more than sufficient for the day in which we live!

4. The Essence of Hosting

A *host* is "a person who receives or entertains guests at home or elsewhere; a person… who provides services, resources, etc." It is to be the host at a dinner or reception, or within one's home or place of gathering.[2]

A host or hostess flows naturally in *hospitality*, which is defined as "the friendly reception and treatment of guests or strangers; the quality of disposition of receiving and treating guests and strangers in a warm, friendly, generous way; kindness and receptiveness in the same manner."[3]

The spiritual gift of hospitality is a healthy connection of the two. One flowing in the gift has a supernatural ability to make people feel comfortable almost instantly. They just know where people are, they have a sense and then an ability to cause people to relax and be at peace.

Hosting is a big deal. It is a ministry unto itself in that, if all that ever happens in any given evening is that people feel genuinely at peace because of their surroundings, then it has been a successful time. A good host or hostess is anticipatory, they are both sensitive to and aware of the needs of those around them. This results in people feeling relaxed and warm emotionally. He/she makes people feel welcomed and valued. This is very important in setting the tone, the mood, for the evening. But not just for one evening. A good hostess makes people feel like wanting to come back. It seems like the coffee pot is always on and there's a pot of chili already to warm and serve! In a spiritual sense, it is truly a piece of the heart of Jesus being expressed.

A spiritual gift is a manifestation of Holy Spirit enabling one to minister to the needs of those present, within or without the Church, as the Spirit directs. It is a gift of grace and an anointed action. The spiritual gift of hospitality operates in a person who has an open house, an open heart, and a warm welcome to those present. The one operating in this gift ministers not just to physical needs but also to emotional and heart needs as the Spirit leads. All are called to be hospitable, but not all operate in the gift of hospitality.

People with any of these spiritual gifts fit well into this ministry: hospitality, serving, helps, exhortation, leadership, mercy, or administration.

5. The Essence of Worship

The word *worship* from Scripture offers several meanings that all come to the same place. It means, "To bow down, to lie prostrate, to honor and revere, an acknowledgement of divine perfection."[4] It also means, "The giving of adoring reverence, to glorify, idolize and praise." All of these meanings come down to the overpowering acknowledgement of the one true God. We do this as a response because he is worthy of it. When we realize over and over again what he has done for us, it is a natural response to not only thank him but to be overwhelmed with thanksgiving and gratitude. And this forever more.

Worship is a heart expression, a heart occurrence. True worship is deep calling out to deep. (Psalm 42:7) It is the depth of the human heart, the human spirit, longing and aching for the depth of the heart of God in intimate connection. It is not about a song, or a song service. It is not even necessarily about music. It is an intimate spiritual expression and resultant connection with the Triune God. There is a sensitivity to Holy Spirit present so as to flow and adjust to his lead. It is vital. We were made for this. Humans need the presence of God; we don't do well without it, without him.

Worship needs to be real, honest, transparent, and vulnerable intimacy, with Father, with Jesus, and with Holy Spirit. The invitation is to be overwhelmed in love and passion for him. And then allow him to overwhelm you with his love for you. Take a risk. Intimacy is risky business. By design. The more risk we take the richer it becomes, the more fulfilled we are in him. He demands to be worshipped; he is worthy of it. If we don't worship him, even the rocks will cry out. (Luke 19:38-40) The demand is not one of pride or arrogance. It is one of desire, his for us. He wants us abandoned, not from him but into him.

Worship is one of the Four Elements for good reason. The more we engage in the heart attitude of worship, the closer we become to him. It is there that we best sense him and hear him. It is there that we best serve him. And the fruit from all that is more than marvelous. Do not minimize it. Bring it to the Gathering. Insist on it. It is absolutely essential!

People with any of these spiritual gifts fit well into this ministry: worship, serving, exhortation, leadership, prophecy, or shepherd.

6. Born Pregnant

One of the inherent problems with any small group model in the US is that they tend to stagnate or die in six to twelve months. This is primarily because there is no element of multiplication established within the parameters of the group. Everyone gets to know each other fairly well, and there is no *fresh blood*, no new people coming in, so it stagnates. In the Gathering model every group is *born pregnant*. If there is actually the intention of expanding, of multiplying Gatherings, then this is an absolutely critical component. Holy Spirit brought this to me many years back. He is quite the Teacher! It is amazing to me just how simple it is, how profound it is – and how well it works!

It comes from an old Star Trek episode called "Trouble with Tribbles." The Enterprise became infested with "tribbles," which were cute little friendly and furry creatures; they were everywhere! The entire episode was spent discovering and dealing with these little guys. By installment's end it was not determined just what they were or even where they came from, but it was discovered that the reason they multiplied so rapidly was because they were *born pregnant*!

The Lord is genius! In this context, what he was saying is that every Home Gathering is started with a leader – and with the leader of the next Gathering already identified and present. This is huge. It means there is no longer a struggle with the development of leadership. When leadership is already established, the expansion goes much smoother and the transition is close to seamless. This carries forward from Gathering to Gathering. So, a group cannot expand until it has identified the leader of the next group; this for each and every multiplication. When Charlie multiplies, he assigns leadership to the new group, to George. And before George can start the group, he must locate and secure the leader for the next one. And Charlie must also locate and secure the leader for his next multiplication. And on.

The unfortunate reality in the Church at large is that there is a serious leadership crisis. This has been going on for multitudes of decades.

The actions behind the born pregnant principle bring a natural focus on leadership to the forefront.

By doing this the value and importance of leadership is emphasized and enhanced. It becomes more of a focus, more talked about, more prayed into, and more sought out. When this happens, the practicality of it gains momentum and purpose. When the Lord is front and center here, when he is invited in to lead and provide, wonderful things happen! When leadership is accentuated, its value, perceived and real, accelerates. When leadership training is offered, it provides the people needed. Simple. Efficient. Effective. All Jesus.

There are times, perhaps and especially in the early stages of building a network, when this component of Gatherings will not work. The network is not large enough or strong enough to support it. Don't sweat it. Holy Spirit is the one we follow. He will direct your path, especially if you keep it a matter of prayer.

7. Transferable

All that we are considering and establishing within the concepts and actualities of the development of Gatherings must be highly transferable. This is absolutely essential. I am defining transferable in this context as having been built in such a manner that it is easily duplicatable. A primary principle within God's Kingdom has to do with everything being about him, and from that about others. As has been previously stated, we must see and understand that it is never about us. Within this understanding is found the truth that as we esteem others more highly than self, we help others to grow and become all that the Father has in mind for them. By making it not only transferable, but perpetually transferable, we are strongly contributing to the advancement of the Kingdom – and God's people within his Kingdom.

For example, if I am holding too tightly to what is being built, then I am actually quenching the Spirit of God and limiting what he desires to do. He is the architect, and his vision is considerably larger than mine. I must seriously resist the temptation to gain and maintain control. I must work at giving away all that he has been so gracious to give me. There are a number of times in the flow of life where we can tend to complicate things. Let's work at not doing that!

8. We Meet Weekly

The key understanding here is commitment. Meeting every week makes a significant statement to all who are involved or are contemplating becoming involved, "We are here for you." Rain or shine, hot or cold, feeling good or feeling bad, it matters not. Press in to the Lord and get the grace, strength, courage, and perspective you need and be involved. Especially if you are in leadership! Remember, they will follow your lead, for better or worse.

I wonder how many of us have had the experience wherein we had absolutely no desire to go to Gathering on a particular night. And everything that can is working to help you stay home. And yet you find it within yourself, probably with the Lord's help whether you sense it or not, and get there. And then later are amazed at how powerful it was for you! I call it the "bathtub syndrome." We raised four children. It happened all the time: You can't get them in the bathtub – and then you can't get them out!

The average church attendee shows up around seventy-five to eighty percent of the time. It is the same in small group ministry. If you meet every other week, that means that person will be there only three weeks out of eight. If you meet monthly, it becomes three times in sixteen. It has been said and it is true, "You cannot have quality without quantity." Said another way, if you want quality, you must have quantity. Gatherings are all about relationships and one can simply not build quality without the quantity of weekly meetings. 'Nuf said.

9. We Bless the Church

We are not apart from the Church, we are simply a different expression of it. It does not belong to us so it is critical that we do not criticize or stand in judgment of it, but rather bless it and be blessed by it. The truth is, it belongs to the Father. (Ephesians 2:19, 20;1; Thessalonians 1:1; 1 Timothy 3:15) Jesus said that he would build it. (Matthew 16:18) It eventually will become the bride of Christ. (2 Corinthians 11:2; Revelation 19:7, 22:17) There are Christians and non-Christians in it. That is for Father to deal with. There are relatively healthy, and very hurt and wounded people in it. That is for Father to deal with. There are some who are free and some who are bound. That is for Father to deal with. He may very well, and often does, choose to work through us in his dealings - but that needs to be at his calling, prompting, and leading and not our own. It may look like a mess. It may look like something other than what you or I would have built had we had the opportunity, or it may be dysfunctional at large. It is still the Father's, and we honor him by honoring what is his.

Oh, by the way, it is dysfunctional because it is full of *people -- human beings just like you and me*! There is only one who is functional and that would be Jesus. The rest of us are in dire need of a savior and do not have the right to pass judgment.

10. Forsake not the Assembling

We are called on to, "Forsake not the assembling of the saints as is the custom of some." (Hebrews 10:25) The word translated *assembling* is akin to sunago, which was talked about in chapter ten. One of the base meanings for sunago is "to assemble, to assemble together."[4] The word is "assembling together."[5] "The term here should be understood as simply the regular gathering together of Christian believers for worship and exhortation in a particular place."[6] "As it was the norm to gather both corporately and from house to house this command from the writer of Hebrews speaks to both. It has been said that the entire book of Hebrews was written to and for an existing house church, [or in our context a Home Gathering."][7] (Brackets mine)

It needs to be seen and understood that the current application, exercised by many, that uses this passage to insist people go to church is, in fact, a misapplication of the text. Assembling is the operative word. Gathering. Sunago. There is no clear connection in this passage to church as we know it at all.

That having been said, any way one looks at it, we are called to assemble. There is no room for the independent, proud, arrogant, rebellious, angry-at-the-Church mentality. Remember that independence is nothing more than the right mix of pride and rebellion. These are things that, through the process of sanctification, the Lord is trying to work out of us! Our call is to humility and submission, which are the exact opposites of pride and rebellion.

Unfortunately, there has been an element within the house church movement, especially in the Unites States, that is strong on independence. That is not the Biblical pattern, nor the will of the Lord. This is not to say there is no room for the ones caught in this mindset. It is to say there is a call and a challenge to an ongoing working within the heart to change this attitude to one that aligns with the heart of the Father for his people and his Church. First

Corinthians 14:26 says, "When you come together…," not if you come together. See also 1 Corinthians 12:27.

11. Children

Each Gathering should handle the care of children as seems right amongst them. Include them in worship if possible. Include them in fellowship, or part of it, as it flows. Some Gatherings have chosen to include the kids in the whole evening every week. Do what works for your Gathering. And don't be afraid to mix it up once in a while. Establish workers for the children from within the group, or bring someone in. Pay them well. Use money from the weekly offering or from a different source. We have had people volunteer to pay for the child care team from their own pocket. Children are a very important part of the whole, so ministry to and with them is equally important. Don't discount them. Make it interesting. Make it fun. Make it full of Holy Spirit. Children are sensitive creatures and can hear and be used by Holy Spirit as much as anybody – and sometimes more!

I think Wolfgang Simson captures the dynamics of children in ministry well:

> "Since house churches are spiritual families, children are a natural and important part of that body, just as they are a source of constant joy – and occasionally embarrassment – in a natural family. Children humble us with their questions, break up our endless 'adult' discussions, bring us down to earth from our pious clouds, and act as natural evangelists and bridge-builders. They also help us to prove the fruits of the Spirit – patience, for example – and serve as heaven-sent spies to spot instantly any trace of religious superstition and hypocrisy. Children have a ministry to us adults that is at least as important

as our ministry to them. They are, in short, as important to house churches as they are to families."[8]

People with any of these spiritual gifts fit well into this ministry: serving, helps, exhortation, leadership, mercy, or administration.

12. Problems with People: Conflict Resolution

Conflict is as common as dirt! It is an inevitable part of life for all of us. Ignoring it will not make it go away, it will actually make it worse. The best thing to do with conflict is to learn how to manage it in a strong and healthy manner. To bring appropriate solutions to conflictual situations brings emotional and mental strength and maturity to all parties involved.

Conflict resolution must be based on the reality that we are not looking for one who is right and one who is wrong. We are not dealing with fault or blame. If it gets reduced to that we will never come to resolution. The tendency toward competition must be seen and eliminated in order to come to the place of resolution and closure. *The ability to agree to disagree is imperative.* The practical realities of patience and tolerance, of humility and the fruits of the Spirit, must be fully activated in order for resolve and forgiveness to flow. We are dealing with differences of opinion here. Period and the end. That is huge!

We are all entitled to our own opinions, right, wrong, or otherwise. As followers of Christ, we have the responsibility to honor others. All others. Whether we agree with them or not. (Romans 12:10, 13:7) Make it your ambition to lead a quiet life and mind your own business. (1 Thessalonians 4:11) Esteem others more highly than yourself. (Philippians 2:3) Determine to defer, to yield, to others.

What an opportunity we have with resolving conflict! Iron does indeed sharpen iron. (Proverbs 27:17) Can we all learn how to get the log out of our own eye and then get the speck out of our brother's or sister's eye? (Matthew 7:3-5) Can we learn to simply own our own, to acknowledge our own challenges, struggles, and weaknesses, and allow the other to do the same? My sin is no better or no worse than yours. We all need a Savior – every day! You are not and you are never, the change agent. That job is already taken; it belongs to Holy Spirit. Pride, arrogance, and its sister stubbornness, are quite unattractive on anyone.

All conflict needs to be addressed at the level at which it occurs. Whatever that level may be, no matter how awkward it may be. Said another way, we must keep short accounts with each other. Matthew 5:23 says, "If you are offering your gift at the altar and there remember that your brother has something against you, leave your gift there in front of the altar. First go and be reconciled to your brother; then come and offer your gift." Mark 11:25 says, "When you stand praying, if you hold anything against anyone, forgive them, so that your Father in heaven may forgive you your sins." So, whether you hold against your brother or he against you, go to him and be reconciled. Either way, your responsibility is to make the move toward the other for the purpose of reconciliation. Judgment and unforgiveness will be handled harshly by Father God. He is slow to judge and quick to forgive; he requires the same from us.

If Sam and Joe have conflict and it is left unresolved, it is required of them, no matter who started it, to work it out one-on-one. If they have that conflict and Sarah and John were present, then they must work it out in their presence. If so, it can be resolved – with no residue, with true closure. If not, then those residuals remain – and will rise up another day to do damage, having been exacerbated by the devil. If this conflict is experienced within the entire group, no matter the size, it must be resolved within that group.

These statements are imperative for the present and future health and well-being of the group and all within it. It is very important to understand that the conflict between these two gentlemen, in the presence of others, may have caused struggle in someone else's heart other than just them. This must be addressed. In this latter example, it would be sufficient for Sam and Joe to resolve their conflict and then bring that resolve to the entire group. As long as there can be clear and healthy understanding and resolution, and from that closure. For all. The point is honest and sincere solution. Then the enemy has no ground, no leverage. (John 14:30) Herein lies a major stumbling block within the Church and our country at large. Cancel culture is not of God; to the contrary, it is evil and must not be allowed to live amongst us. In Christ, let's learn to be mature about life.

> *"The closer and longer we walk with God,*
> *the more we do battle with him."*

That battle has to do with the inner-man issues we have and that God will bring up for the greater purpose of healing.

In the overall context of group dynamics, it is essential to learn the nuances of dealing with what I call the EGR. Allow me to explain. In the world of automobiles, in the interest of reducing emissions, there was once a valve called an exhaust gas recirculation valve, commonly referred to as an EGR valve. Its purpose was to recirculate hot exhaust gases back into the air/fuel intake manifold to cool things down, thin things out, and thus eliminate nitrous oxides from forming and polluting the air. Think hot, usually thin air circulating in a constant state.

The EGR is that person who chooses to emit what amounts to hot air in waxing eloquent about his or her pet peeve or superior knowledge about some subject. They are labeled an EGR because there is Extra Grace Required to handle them! They often know it all, and if you doubt that, just ask them and they will assure you of this fact! They tend to dominate the conversations at the expense of all those around them. Truth be told, all of us have been that person on some level at one time or another, perhaps still. Let grace abound. But this situation must be handled before it quenches the whole group and Holy Spirit in your midst. This phenomenon has been known to absolutely kill a Gathering. People refuse to come back because of Mr. EGR. He is toxic. Don't let that happen!

There are several "tricks of the trade" that can be used effectively. The first is to allow the group to handle the situation. Often there are those in the group who are strong enough to confront with grace and tact, and can stop the situation before it gets out of hand. The second, as the leader, is to redirect. Wait for Mr. EGR to take a breath (sometimes, literally, this is the only way into his hot air expulsion) and immediately ask someone else what their thought on the subject matter is. It is usually best if that someone is the assistant leader, or someone who is privy to what you are doing. That is because our EGR may not be affected by the redirect and will attempt to override it. Are we having fun yet? Another form of redirect is to accomplish it yourself by either asking a different question or injecting some of your own thought on the subject. In any case, be sure to avoid all eye contact with EGR during this interchange.

If necessary, the next step is to approach the person directly. This should be done one-on-one immediately after the evening is over. With full eye contact, explain clearly and concisely exactly what has just transpired. Be direct and brief. Bring the history of it. Allow him to rebut, but be clear that it is not to happen again. He is valuable, his input is valuable, but so is everyone else's. He needs to learn how to honor and respect all those around him. And then pray with him. Do realize that at the core of this behavior is a wounded person that has been challenged and usually has very low social skills.

If it happens again, then go through the process again, giving EGR the benefit of the doubt and a double dose of mercy and grace. This will also help him know the seriousness of the offense.

Then if it happens again, it will be necessary to call him out immediately in the context of the offense. Don't wait for a more convenient time, there won't be one. It is never convenient to have to do this. It can be very helpful and healthy if managed properly. Pray for that. He may very well be quite embarrassed and over-react. Be prepared for that. Resist argumentation. Redirect again. As difficult as this can be, if he does not stop require him to leave. Then pray with the group for him and never against him. Perhaps he will simply be quiet and then never return. If that is the case, be sure to follow up with him in a few weeks. If possible, leave the door open. At some point he may yield, break, and be healed. I have several good friends that were once EGR's in my Gatherings. He just hurts and needs a friend. When you get right down to it, he is really no different than you or me. We all need help, a friend, and a Savior.

13. The Oikos Principle. This is How we Grow!

The great majority of people who come to Christ are brought to him by ordinary people – friends, neighbors, co-workers, and relatives – who take a genuine interest in them. They serve them, share their lives with them, and eventually share the Gospel. This is the most natural and effective method of evangelism.

There is a Greek word *oikos*. It has a handful of variants that translate into English as house, household, family, home, market, or members of one's household. A bigger perspective easily translates the concept as an extended network of relationships, or a sphere or circle of influence. We all have a *circle of influence*. It is this circle that is the focal point of the *oikos* principle.

My circle of influence consists of my extended family, the people I am friends with, the people I hang out with, the people I see on a regular basis. The neighbor I wave to but have never had any meaningful conversation with is not in my *oikos*. But the neighbor I see and talk with regularly is. The grocery person I look for and purpose to interact with so as to build relationship is in my *oikos*; the one I see once or twice but have no connection with is not.

This is quite evident in Scripture. For example, in Acts 16:15, we see Lydia and the members of her household coming to Jesus. In Acts 16:31-33, we see the Philippian jailer and his household coming to Christ. Cornelius, all his family, his relatives, and his close friends all came to right relationship with Jesus in Acts 10:1-2, 22-24. In Matthew 9:10 we see Matthew, along with many tax collectors and sinners coming to Jesus! The early church used personal relationships as bridges to Jesus.

This pattern is our pattern to follow within our *oikos,* our circle of influence. Effective, natural outreach flows through our *oikos.*

This is actually a very fun and freeing manner of evangelism. When we understand that the one, true Evangelist is Holy Spirit, we can relax, be free of all guilt and expectations to bring everyone we see to Jesus, and simply flow with Holy Spirit and watch him work! There are several simple steps to take to build an entire mindset, and resultant ministry, out of this: Identify your *oikos,* couple with others in your Gathering to consistently pray for yours and theirs, look for the opportunities that the Lord will bring as a result of the prayers – and he will -- and keep it up!

The prayer is that the Lord would reveal his love for these people through you. Not by way of some heavy preaching or attempts at arguing folks to God. But by way of expressions of love and care.

How simple is that?! How fun is it, to be used by God to share his kindness? Engage those in your circle of influence. Listen to what they are saying, with their mouths and hearts. Bring that to Gathering to be shared and prayed into with others doing the same. And then look for the opportunities to love others with the love of Jesus. Keep it up and see what Holy Spirit will accomplish through you! The *Oikos* Principle. It truly is how we grow!

14. Out There

Research suggests that approximately ten percent of any group of believers will operate in the spiritual gift of evangelism. The rest of us often just operate under some form of guilt! The Church at large has done us all a disservice by attempting to attach an unreasonable, unbiblical expectation regarding the saving of souls. Paul said, "I have become all things to all people that I might save some." (1 Corinthians 9:22) Very poor translation. Paul saved no one. That is God's job, and in all reality, it is Holy Spirit who is the evangelist.

Father, please release us all from the guilt and shame we have received from errant teachings and expectations. Replace that with your love and heart for us. Teach us how to follow your ideas, intentions, and directives regarding evangelism, and to be at peace in that. In Jesus' name we pray.

We do, however, have an assignment from the Lord. From Matthew 22:37-40 we are called to love God, love our neighbor, and love ourselves. Love in these verses is *agape*, which is a determined act of the will. It is a command from his heart to ours. A significant part of this love has to do with caring for and investing in others. This is what *Out There* is all about.

In his book, *Conspiracy of Kindness*, Steve Sjogren shares how a fellowship full of small groups evangelized a city. They, "operate on one simple premise: that God is passionately in love with unbelievers and can win them most effectively through acts of kindness."[11] It says in Romans 2:4 that it is, "the kindness of God that leads people to repentance." These people built an entire ministry around that passage – and took over a city! They created small groups that met regularly and went into the pool halls and bird watching clubs, the neighborhoods and the malls, simply to perform acts of kindness for people with no strings attached. In the back of the book there is a list of fifty-eight different projects they took on, all on a regular basis, and that in the midst of a list of hundreds of ideas for this type of outreach. Oil changes for single moms, outdoor window washing for elderly folks, rainy/snowy day grocery escort service – helping people navigate wet and slippery parking lots. The list goes on. Yard work, light home repair, smoke detector battery replacement, dog-doo clean up. All this done regularly with a heart to serve, with a heart of compassion. Oh, and always free with no donations or tips accepted.

A powerful component of this endeavor is that it is all done without the initial mention of Jesus or Church. It is not about either. It is not about trying to build something, except the building of the hearts of others by way of an act of kindness. Introducing Jesus into the conversations came later, after an arena of trust had been built.

Powerful. And, if considered in the heart in which it's intended, fun and fulfilling for all.

Put this into the schedule of your Gathering every four to six weeks and see what happens to the hearts of your people and your city.

People still need people. Eye contact is still the best form of comfort and encouragement. The ministry of presence is amazingly powerful.

People with any of these spiritual gifts fit well into this ministry: leadership, serving, helps, exhortation, mercy, administration, prophecy, words of knowledge, or intercession.

15. Things to do Together

This principle helps tremendously in breaking the ice and melding hearts together. There is nothing like an afternoon of volleyball or softball to bring a group of people together. Throw in some hot dogs and potato salad and you have a recipe for delight -- and success in relationship building. Be creative. Energize your creative folks and let them run with it. And be aware that other people are watching. They are drawn to the camaraderie, to the joy and laughter, to the delight they are witnessing. Watch out, it might draw some of them in for meaningful conversation! Schedule this often.

People with any of these spiritual gifts fit well into this ministry: leadership, serving, helps, exhortation, mercy, administration, or hospitality.

16. Considering Money

Tithes and offerings are founded in the Scriptures, Old and New Testament. (Genesis 14:20,28:22; Leviticus 27:30; Malachi 3:10) God looks on the heart, and one can measure where their heart is by where their money is. (Matthew 6:19-21) As well, the New Testament makes it clear that God is a very generous God, and he loves when we follow his lead and are the same. (Luke 6:38; 2 Corinthians 9:6-9) All members of any given Home Gathering are encouraged and directed to be obedient to the Lord in this.

All money is given to the Corporation, a 501(c)3 entity. Tithes and offerings are collected weekly. All money collected is to be redistributed as per the Constitution and By-laws of said Corporation. As there will be little or no building expenses and minimal people needing a salary, overhead should be minimal. Typical overhead would include such things as travel and related expenses for those moving about the network(s), insurance coverages as needed for each Home Gathering, paid leaders and administrators (if any), and administrative and material expenses.

All other money would be channeled back into Home Gathering outreach and activities, benevolence, and the like. The leader of each Home Gathering is the responsible party for collection of money coming into their Gathering. All money would go to the Corporate Treasurer, and never directly from and back to people within the Gathering. This is all to be done formally with documentation. This is also how giving becomes tax deductible, for those who desire. This procedure is to be delegated by the leader to another within the Home Gathering, not his or her spouse. The money would go through the Treasurer for proper documentation and then on to distribution back to the Gathering leaders as need arises. If all are faithful and obedient, it is anticipated that there will be significant money to use for the advancement of the Kingdom.

17. Spiritual Covering

This is grossly underplayed in western Christianity. The spiritual dynamics are way more powerful and significant than they are understood to be. Imagine with me an open umbrella which has several holes, thus rendering it less than fully effective in its purpose. The umbrella represents a covering from the rain. But more than that, it characterizes a spiritual covering over a person, family, geographic area, or a ministry. The umbrella is the Spirit of God hovering over that person, covering them from the fiery darts of the evil one. (Genesis 1:2; Job 37:16; Ephesians 6:16) 1 Peter 5:8 says, "Be alert and of sober mind. Your adversary, the devil, prowls around like a roaring lion, seeking someone to devour." John 10:10a says, "The thief comes only to steal and kill and destroy..." The umbrella, the covering, protects those under it from evil, from harm, from the many things the devil will throw at them. The holes in the umbrella represent issues of sin or iniquity. These are things done by or to you or yours, bondages or strongholds that open the door and give the enemy the right to be there and occupy, and do as much damage as possible.

So, if you attempt to take ground for the King in his Kingdom, personally or with a group and you are not covered, not connected to an authority higher than yourself, you will be like one of the sons of Sceva in Acts 19:13-16. It was an ugly scene when they tried to overcome a demon while operating outside of their covering. The enemy wants you dead. It is that simple. And that scary when one is not in proper alignment. Yet, on the other hand, when that umbrella has no holes in it – because the holes are covered by another of more authority – the enemy has no play.

Please don't get ahead of this dialogue. The ultimate covering is the ultimate authority and his name is Jesus. I am not suggesting otherwise. Within that truth and understanding, it is important to see that there is an order of things, a hierarchy. God chooses to anoint and empower some people with more authority than others.

It is his call, his choice. The story of the centurion and his sick slave in Mathew 8:5-10 and again in Luke 7:1-10 speaks clearly of the dynamic of levels of authority. If we can receive and settle into that reality, it goes much better for us. Certain people have chosen to grab that authority without it being given. For them, it has, or will, end up like Sceva's sons. On the other hand, for those who choose to walk in brokenness and humility with their God, he gives an increase. This is not earned or performed into. It is his will, choice, and determination.

Receive this, or not, it is your choice. But before you blow this off, look around you and see the beauty of the Lord on one hand and the devastation of the enemy on the other. Get covered. Be covered. Stay covered. Your resistance to this, your independence is nothing more than the right mix of pride and rebellion -- and tremendous fodder for the devil. Resist the temptation. Refuse to be an island or a lone ranger.

We are created for community, for relationships; your covering ought to be found there. Otherwise, you become foodstuff for the enemy. Remember, it is not just a covering, it is a spiritual covering. It is based on relationships, both vertical and horizontal. It has nothing to do with money. It has nothing to do with title, label, or ordination. Although, the latter may become one of the results of things over time.

CHAPTER NINETEEN

THOUGHTS AND INSIGHTS FROM THE TRENCHES

What follows is a culmination of observations and understandings which come from the many years I have spent building and leading Home Gatherings. Some of them are more astute in nature, while others have a more practical application. All of them have been beneficial in learning and growing in the dynamics of life with Jesus in a small group environment.

- It is often in the midst of relationships (gone bad) that we get hurt. It is always in the midst of relationships (centered in Christ) that we get healed.

- Whether it happened and you didn't want it to or it didn't and you did – either way it equals heartache.

- This thing we call life with Jesus, with the Father, and with Holy Spirit is not about catering to our weaknesses; they are ever present. It is about building our strengths. He is about building, developing, and re-generating us.

- Remember, it is only drama if you make it drama.

- Character: The sum total of ALL your everyday choices.

- Integrity: What you do/who you are when no one is around.

- "Pray to the Lord for it; because if it prospers you too will prosper." (Jeremiah 29:7)

- If you allow circumstances to control you, then you will walk in defeat. If you will allow the Spirit of God to rise up in you and direct your path, then you will walk in victory.

- The Lord said to me, "Sharing with me, bringing your thoughts, ideas, struggles, and dilemmas to me, moment by moment, brings a peace that you will know no other way. Be sensitive to the promptings of my Spirit in this regard."

- Get up and stand. Stand strong and fight. Fight hard and win – in the name of Jesus.

- "It doesn't matter, really, how great the pressure is. It only matters where the pressure lies. See that it never comes between you and the Lord. Then the greater the pressure, the more it presses you to his breast."[1]

- "Every force that has been at work will tell of God's purposes in the end."[2]

- Remember: "Make it your ambition to lead a quiet life – and mind your own business." (1 Thessalonians 4:11)

- "For anxiety breeds tension, and tension erodes joy. And when joy is gone victory is lost, faith is weakened, and spontaneity is destroyed."[3]

- "God's activity upon me is the guarantee of the value he places in me and of the ultimate intention he has for me."[4]

- Jesus is:

- The man of sorrows (Isaiah 5:3)
- The God of victory (Isaiah 2:8)
- And it is all for us (Acts 2:39)

- It is not the love *for* Christ that is the motivator. In all honesty, that will not get you very far. It is the love that comes *from* Christ that stirs and drives and energizes.

- Busyness is a form of mistrust. Mistrust is rooted in fear. Fear is what stands in the way.

- Relationship is not based on what you are doing – but rather on whom you are pursuing.

- Sometimes life is a jigsaw puzzle - seemingly without borders!

- "I will forgive their wickedness and will remember their sins no more." (Jeremiah 31:34b) The Father, Son, and Holy Spirit, with a heart of love and compassion, want all to know of their great mercy.

- Faith and trust are twin brothers.

- Faith is truly spelled R-I-S-K.[5]

- Ours is to plant and water. God supplies the increase. (1 Corinthians 3:6 KJV)

- We cannot appropriately minister out of our *need*, only from our *surplus*. The former is about *get* and comes from our weaknesses and wounds; the latter is about *give* and derives from our strengths and security in Christ.

- We all need:

- a touch
- a hug
- a listening ear
- affirmation
- encouragement
- understanding
- someone to hold our hand

- In over forty years of ministry, one of the biggest mistakes I ever made was the time I missed the road signs from the Lord. Within my own understanding, agenda, and ambition, I turned a vibrant and healthy "house church" that was ripe and ready to multiply into a "conventional community church." And this complete with the expenditure of a fair amount of money for necessary equipment and supplies. Deep sigh. It failed. We closed the doors within about six months after that move. Not that there is anything wrong with a community church. The mistake was in getting ahead of the Lord, of not listening, not hearing, and therefore not following the Lord's lead.

- "Let your conversation be always full of grace, seasoned with salt, so that you may know how to answer everyone." (Colossians 4:6)

- Small group ministry is intended to be:

  - relational
  - personal
  - encouraging
  - edifying

- Small group ministry is about:

  - listening to God and one another
  - building each other up in the faith

- praying one for another
- sunago/community
- esteeming others higher than yourself
- ministering to others on their level

- Small group ministry is not about:

  - offering counsel. Please do not be offended at this: people are not looking for your counsel, they are looking for God
  - waxing eloquent on your favorite subject
  - listening to yourself carry on

- We want to:

  - avoid being an "EGR"
  - give and receive freely
  - be thoughtful and outward focused as much as possible
  - hear carefully from the Lord and flow accordingly, without attaching self to the prophetic unction

- Success in this kind of ministry, since it is always all about relationships, happens not only on your night of meeting, but from what happens between meetings. Relationships don't build or grow when they are based on a few hours once a week. They quickly become limited and people settle there. *You must pursue others.* Establish some sort of system wherein everyone in the group is being contacted in some manner between meetings. Use your assistant leaders in this. This says you care. This says you are thinking of them. This is important to them.

- You don't know what you have until you have it. Anyone who has hired anyone will tell you, you do not know the caliber or quality of your new employee until after the rubber meets the road. Resumes, interviews, and background checks aside, it is not until Johnny employee has come to work day by day for a while that you can actually measure and assess who and what you have in him. The more genuine and trusting the environment, the smoother, faster, and easier that process is. It all comes down to the individual, the one-on-one connections. To the degree that that is seen, understood, and followed will come the same degree of success. Pick your next leader wisely.

- Cultivate an environment that invites and procures his presence. Praise brings Presence, Presence brings Joy, and the Joy of the Lord is your Strength!

- Cultivate an environment that invites and procures servanthood.

- Learn how to:

  - handle a small group
  - be fluid
  - take appropriate leadership and maintain that
  - maintain the direction of discussion
  - ask questions that give the answer you are looking for so as to keep things moving along

- Find the balance between taking the floor and letting others speak.

- Know how to:

  - intercede
  - do prayer ministry
  - hear God
  - study
  - teach
  - manage

- lead
- follow
- train and release

- Learn to talk with one person while acknowledging another:

  - with eye contact
  - with a touch
  - with a statement
  - by including them in dialogue

- Never, never have fun at someone else's expense. Especially your spouse or children. Banter is okay once respect has been earned and in balance.

- Guard your people in prayer.

- Make continual observations into their lives.

- Find out what the Father is doing. And then do that.

- Follow through:

  - on anything stated or promised
  - on prayer requests
  - whenever you don't see them regularly

- Be a friend. Be a listener. Be a caring person.

- "Let your gentleness be evident to all. The Lord is near." (Philippians 4:5)

- Be someone people can identify with.

- Be someone people are spiritually attracted to. Then point them to Jesus.

- Do prayer ministry often. Keep the prayer groups small.

- You have a responsibility to your group. You have to earn the right to exercise it. Do not presume – you will lose them quickly.

- Think of others first. Put yourself in their shoes. Do for them.

- Any time I am thinking about me I am making a mistake.

- Any time I am making it about me I am making a mistake.

- Know how to handle the newcomer and the wallflower.

- Twelve characteristics of a successful Gathering:

  1. They become a close family.
  2. There is strong application of the Bible to daily life.
  3. There is open and honest sharing of life's ups and downs.
  4. There is effective one-to-one pastoral care by all members.
  5. There is strong encouragement and edification.
  6. There are unlimited opportunities for meaningful service within and outside the group.
  7. There is non-manipulative friendship and servant evangelism.
  8. There is the discipling of new believers.
  9. There is strong evidence of spiritual growth.
  10. There are regular manifestations of the gifts of the Spirit.
  11. There is free, deep, and intimate worship.
  12. There is development of strong leadership.[6]

Life, especially within the camaraderie and intimacy available to us with Father, Jesus, and Holy Spirit, is a journey, rich and wonderful. We do well to see it as such, and not as a destination. Walking along the path that comprises that journey is intended to be the most rewarding and fulfilling experience on the planet. There is no better place to encounter our Lord within that journey than in the heart and wonder of Home Gatherings. It is where we grow, mature, and share the goodness of our God and one another. It does not get any better than that. I hope and trust that this book has aided you in your journey. I pray that you have been both encouraged and equipped to advance the Kingdom of God from within the parameters you have been given in this book. God bless you as you pursue him all the more in the coming months and years.

END NOTES

Chapter Two:

1. Wimber, John. Exact source unknown.
2. Barna Research Group. Exact source unknown.
3. Andersen, Hans Christian. *The Emperor's New Clothes*, common folklore, 1837.
4. Barna, George. *The Frog in the Kettle*. Venture, CA: Regal Books, 1990.
5. Spurgeon, C.H. *The Early Years, 1834-1859*. The Banner of Truth Trust, 1962. Quoted in *Catch the Fire*, Guy Chevreau, Harper Collins Publishers U.K., 1994.
6. Simson, Wolfgang. *The House Church Book*. Carol Stream, IL: BarnaBooks, Tyndale House Publishers, Inc, 2009.
7. Tozer, A.W. *The Pursuit of God*. Camp Hill, PA: Christian Publications, 1982.
8. Silvoso, Ed. *Ekklesia*. Minneapolis, MN: Chosen, Baker Publishing Group, 2017.

Chapter Three:

1. Barna, George. *Revolution*, Tyndale House Publishing, Wheaton, IL, 2024.
2. Slife, Dr. Jay. *First Things First*, Revised Edition. Bloomington, IN: WestBow Press, 2024.
3. Guralnik, David B. *New World Dictionary, Second College Edition*. Cleveland, OH: William Collins Publishers, Inc., 1979.
4. Slife, Jay. *My Father's Business: Discipling Nations, Chapter Six*. Clairemont, CA: Wagner University, 2019.
5. Simson, Wolfgang. *The House Church Book*. Carol Stream, IL: Tyndale House Publishers, Inc., 2009.
6. Wimber, John. Exact source unknown.

Chapter Four:

1. Misty Edwards. *IHOP Worship Set*, April 9, 2017
2. Chuck Swindoll. Exact source unknown.
3. Guralnik, David B. *New World Dictionary, Second College Edition*. Cleveland, OH: William Collins Publishers, Inc., 1979.
4. *The New Webster's Encyclopedic Dictionary of the English Language*. New York, NY: Gramercy Books, Random House Value Publishing, Inc., 1997.
5. Slife, Dr. Jay. *First Things First*, First Revised. Edition Bloomington, IN: WestBow Press, 2024.
6. Joyner, Rick. Exact source unknown.
7. Tozer, A.W. *The Pursuit of God*. Camp Hill, PA: Christian Publications, 1982.
8. Zodhiates, Spiro. *The Complete Word Study Dictionary, New Testament*. Chattanooga, TN: AMG Publishers, 1992.

Chapter Five:

1. Slife, Dr. Jay. *First Things First*, Revised Edition. Bloomington, IN: WestBow Press, 2024.
2. Source unknown.
3. Barna, George. *Revolution*. Wheaton, IL: Tyndale House Publishing, 2012.
4. Guralnik, David B. *New World Dictionary, Second College Edition*. Cleveland, OH: William Collins Publishers, Inc., 1979.
5. Slife, Dr. Jay. *First Things First*, Revised Edition. Bloomington, IN: WestBow Press, 2024.

Chapter Six:

1. Slife, Jay. *My Father's Business: Discipling Nations, Chapter Six*. Clairemont, CA: Wagner University, 2019.

2. Slife, Dr. Jay. *First Things First,* Revised Edition. Bloomington, IN: WestBow Press, 2024.
3. Ibid.
4. Wimber, John. Exact source unknown.

Chapter Seven:

1. Bright, John. *The Kingdom of God.* Nashville, TN: Abingdon Press, 1953.
2. Ladd, George Eldon. *The Gospel of the Kingdom.* Grand Rapids, MI: Wm. B. Eerdmans Publishing Co., 1959.
3. Barker, Kenneth. *The NIV Study Bible,* Study Notes. Grand Rapids, MI: Zondervan Bible Publishers, 1985.
4. Ladd, George Eldon. *The Gospel of the Kingdom.* Grand Rapids, MI: Wm. B. Eerdmans Publishing Co., 1959.
5. Ibid.
6. Ibid.
7. Ibid.
8. Ibid.
9. Ibid.
10. Ibid.
11. Ibid.
12. Ibid.
13. Wuest, Kenneth S. *The New Testament: An Expanded Translation.* Grand Rapids, MI: Wm. B. Eerdmans Publishing Co., 1961.
14. Hagner, Donald A. *Word Biblical Commentary, Volume 33A.* Dallas, TX: Word Books, 1993.
15. Bright, John. *The Kingdom of God.* Nashville, TN: Abingdon Press, 1953.

Chapter Eight:

1. Wagner University, Doctor of Apostolic Leadership and Applied Theology. *Church Planting and Church Growth Class, Course Objective.* 2018.

2. Simson, Wolfgang. *The House Church Book*. Carol Stream, IL: Tyndale House Publishers, Inc., 2009.

3. Strong, James. *The New Strong's Exhaustive Concordance of the Bible*, Nashville, TN: Thomas Nelson Publishers, 1990.

4. Simson, Wolfgang. *The House Church Book*. Carol Stream, IL: Tyndale House Publishers, Inc., 2009.

5. Ibid.

6. Zdero, Rad. *The Global House Church Movement*. Pasadena, CA: William Carey Library, 2004.

7. Ibid.

8. Ibid.

9. Ibid.

10. Ibid.

11. Ibid.

12. Wilberforce, William. Revised and Updated by Beltz, Dr. Bob. *Real Christianity*. Minneapolis, MN: Bethany House, Baker Publishing Group, 2006.

Chapter Nine:

1. Guralnik, David B. *New World Dictionary, Second College Edition*. Cleveland, OH: William Collins Publishers, Inc., 1979.

2. Simson, Wolfgang. *The House Church Book*. Carol Stream, IL: Tyndale House Publishers, Inc., 2009.

3. Ibid.

4. Katz, Art. *Apostolic Conversion*. Quoted in Simson, Wolfgang. *The House Church Book*. Carol Stream, IL: Tyndale House Publishers, Inc., 2009.

5. Crabb, Larry. *Connecting*. Nashville, TN: Word Publishing, 1997. Quoted in Simson, Wolfgang. *The House Church Book*. Carol Stream, IL: Tyndale House Publishers, Inc., 2009.

6. Quoted by the unsaved husband of a woman who was part of our Home Gathering.

7. Wimber, John. *Small Group Leadership Development* Notes. Other data unknown.
8. Source unknown.
9. Wagner University, Doctor of Apostolic Leadership and Applied Theology. *Church Planting and Church Growth Class,* 2018.
10. Wimber, John. *Small Group Leadership Development* Notes. Other data unknown.

Chapter Ten:

1. Strong, James. *The New Strong's Exhaustive Concordance of the Bible.* Nashville, TN: Thomas Nelson Publishers, 1990.
2. Ibid.
3. Ibid.
4. Ibid.
5. Goodrick, Edward W. and Kohlenberger III, John R. *Zondervan NIV Exhaustive Concordance.* Grand Rapids, MI: Zondervan Publishing House, 1990.
6. Bauer, Walter. *A Greek-English Lexicon of the New Testament* (BAGD). Chicago, IL: The University of Chicago Press, 1979.
7. Zodhiates, Spiro. *The Complete Word Study Dictionary, New Testament.* Chattanooga, TN: AMG Publishers, 1992.
8. Ibid.
9. Brown, Colin. *The New International Dictionary of New Testament Theology* (NIDNTT). Grand Rapids, MI: Zondervan Publishing House, 1986.
10. Ibid.
11. Ibid.
12. Ibid.

Chapter Eleven:

1. *Dictionary.com,* Rock Holdings, Inc., 2018.

2. Strong, James. *The New Strong's Exhaustive Concordance of the Bible*. Nashville, TN: Thomas Nelson Publishers, 1990.

Chapter Twelve:

1. *Dictionary.com*, Rock Holdings, Inc., 2018.
2. Kohlenberger III, John R., Goodrick, Swanson. *The Greek English Concordance to the New Testament*. Grand Rapids, MI: Zondervan Publishing House, 1997.
3. Wagner, C. Peter. *The Book of Acts, A Commentary*. Minneapolis, MN: Baker Publishing Group, 2017.
4. *Dictionary.com*, Rock Holdings, Inc., 2018.
5. Ibid.

Chapter Fourteen:

1. Source unknown.
2. Source unknown.
3. *Dictionary.com*, Rock Holdings, Inc., 2018.
4. Wimber, John. Exact Source Unknown.
5. *A Systems Model of the Church in Ministry and Mission*. The Center for Parish Development. Other data unknown.
6. Guralnik, David B. *New World Dictionary, Second College Edition*. Cleveland, OH: William Collins Publishers, Inc., 1979.

Chapter Fifteen:

1. Wimber, John. Quoted in Dawson, Connie. *John Wimber: His Life and Ministry*. Lincoln, NE: Self Published, 2020.
2. Source unknown.
3. Blanchard, Ken and Hodges, Hendry. *Lead Like Jesus*. Nashville, TN: W Publishing, 2016.
4. Zodhiates, Spiro. *The Complete Word Study Dictionary, New Testament*. Chattanooga, TN: AMG Publishers, 1992.

5. Ibid.
6. Source unknown.
7. The movie *Gandhi*, 1982.
8. Strong, James. *The New Strong's Exhaustive Concordance of the Bible*. Nashville, TN: Thomas Nelson Publishers, 1990.
9. Ibid.
10. *Dictionary.com*, Rock Holdings, Inc., 2018.

Chapter Sixteen:

1. Eldred, Kenneth A. *God is at Work*. Montrose, CO: Manna Ventures, LLC, 2009.
2. Slife, Jay. *My Father's Business: Discipling Nations, Chapter Six*. Clairemont, CA: Wagner University, 2019.
3. Downing, Sister Laura. "Apostolic Religious: Lay Ecclesial Ministers?". IHM, Boston, MA, April, 2018. [recovered 12-2-2022, 6:00 PM]
4. Ibid.
5. *Dictionary.com*, Rock Holdings, Inc., 2018.
6. Guralnik, David B. *New World Dictionary, Second College Edition*. Cleveland, OH: William Collins Publishers, Inc., 1979.
7. *The New Webster's Encyclopedic Dictionary of the English Language*. New York, NY: Gramercy Books, Random House Value Publishing, Inc., 1997.

Chapter Seventeen:

1. Source unknown.
2. Source unknown.

Chapter Eighteen:

1. Engle, Lou. *The Jesus Fast*. Bloomington, MN: Chosen Books, 2016.

2. *Dictionary.com*, Rock Holdings, Inc., 2018.
3. Ibid.
4. Exact source unknown. This definition follows very closely to the one found in Strong, James. *The New Strong's Exhaustive Concordance of the Bible*. Nashville, TN: Thomas Nelson Publishers, 1990.
5. Ibid.
6. Strong, James. *The New Strong's Exhaustive Concordance of the Bible*. Nashville, TN: Thomas Nelson Publishers, 1990.
7. Ibid.
8. Rogers, Jr., Cleon L. and Rogers III, Cleon L. *The New Linguistic and Exegetical Key to the Greek New Testament*. Grand Rapids, MI: Zondervan Publishing House, 1998.
9. Martin, Ralph P. and Davids, Peter H. *Dictionary of the Later New Testament and its Developments*. Downers Grove, IL: InterVarsity Press, 1997.
10. Simson, Wolfgang. *The House Church Book*. Carol Stream, IL: Tyndale House Publishers, Inc., 2009.
11. Swindoll, Chuck. Exact source unknown.
12. George, Carl F. *Prepare Your Church for the Future*. Grand Rapids, MI: Fleming H Revell, Baker Book House, 1992.
13. Sjogren, Steve. *Conspiracy of Kindness*. Ann Arbor, MI: Servant Publications, 1993.

Chapter Nineteen:

1. Taylor, Hudson. Exact source unknown.
2. Chambers, Oswald. *My Utmost for His Highest*. New York, NY: Dodd, Mead and Company, 1935.
3. Source unknown.
4. Source unknown.
5. Wimber, John. Exact source unknown.
6. Source unknown.

Recommended Reading: (Ordered by Title, Subtitle, Author, Publisher, and Copyright)

201 Great Questions, Jerry D. Jones, NavPress, 1992.

A Tale of Three Kings, A Study in Brokenness, Gene Edwards, Tyndale House Publishers Inc., 1992.

Conspiracy of Kindness, A Refreshing New Approach to Sharing the Love of Jesus with Others, Steve Sjogren, Servant Publications, 1993.

Ekklesia, Rediscovering God's Instrument for Global Transformation, Ed Silvoso, Chosen Books, 2017.

Finding God, Dr. Larry Crabb, 1993.

First Things First, Revised Edition, Navigating Our Challenging Times through the Words of Jesus, Dr. Jay Slife, WestBow Press, 2024.

God's Promises for Your Every Need, J. Countryman Division, Word Publishing Inc., 1995.

Humility, The Journey Toward Holiness, Andrew Murray, Bethany House, 2001.

Keeping the Fire, Discovering the Heart of True Revival, Rolland Baker, Chosen Books, 2016.

Lead Like Jesus Revisited, Lessons from the Greatest Leadership Role Model of all Time, Blanchard, Hodges, and Hendry, W Publishing, 2016.

Miscarriage of a Dream, What to Do When God's Plans Don't Match Yours, Kristi Larrabee, Author Academy Elite, 2020.

The Global House Church Movement, Rad Zdero, William Carey Library, 2004.

The Gospel of the Kingdom, Popular Expositions on the Kingdom of God, George Eldon Ladd, Eerdmans Publishing Company, 1959.

The House Church Book, Rediscover the Dynamic, Organic, Relational, Viral Community Jesus Started, Wolfgang Simson, Barna, 2009.

The Knowledge of the Holy, A. W. Tozer, HarperOne, 1961.

The Making of a Leader, Second Edition, Recognizing the Lessons and Stages of Leadership Development, Dr. J. Robert Clinton, NavPress, 2012

The Pursuit of God, The Human Thirst for the Divine, A. W. Tozer, Christian Publications Inc., 1993.

True Faced, Trust God and Others with Who You Really Are, Experience Edition, Thrall, McNicol, Lynch, NavPress, 2004.

Well Versed, Biblical Answers to Today's Tough Issues, James L Garlow, Regnery Publishing, 2016.

Printed in the United States
by Baker & Taylor Publisher Services